THE COURT, THE ATLANTIC AND THE CITY

The Court, the Atlantic and the City

Sir Walter Ralegh v William Sanderson

MICHAEL FRANKS

with a foreword by
Mr John Wingfield Digby of Sherborne Castle

First published in the United Kingdom in 2009
by South and West Books, Field House, Mapledurwell, Hants RG25 2LU

ISBN 978-0-9562683-0-3
Printed and bound in Great Britain by
CPI Antony Rowe, Chippenham and Eastbourne
Typeset in 11/12.5pt Bembo
Typesetting and origination by Ian Taylor, www.taylorthorne.co.uk

Foreword

Since my ancestor Sir John Digby acquired Sherborne in 1617 the family has always been very conscious that the estate and Sherborne Lodge (Ralegh's new house, pictured on the back cover of the book and now incorporated within Sherborne Castle) have provided a direct, surviving, physical link with him. So I am delighted to write a Foreword to Michael Franks' book.

William Sanderson, a comparatively unknown merchant from the City of London married Ralegh's niece in 1584, became a close friend of his uncle-in-law and acted as his man of business and banker. For some ten years he enabled Ralegh to realize his ambitious plans until they quarreled over the funding of Ralegh's first expedition to Guyana, undertaken to find the fabulous wealth of El Dorado.

Although the working connection was terminated – and some years later the parties went to law over their quarrel – the social relationship between the Raleghs and the Sandersons continued, ending only with a visit to the prison on the night before Ralegh's execution in 1618.

Ralegh was a very unusual man, with many brilliant and attractive qualities, but also with some flaws, in particular difficulties over inter-personal relationships. He had "insufferable pride" and showed poor judgment of other people. Further, with his powerful intellect and tendency to question everything, he was perceived as a trouble-maker, and indeed, acquired – contrary to the truth – the reputation of a non-believer. This mix of characteristics, and perhaps also the difference in social rank, played their part in the mercurial relationship between the two men.

In this book Michael Franks has combined an account of what the two men achieved together with an analysis of the personal chemistry between them – something which I believe has not been done before. I found the mixture of fact and opinion fascinating and I hope that you too will find it interesting.

I also hope that you may find an opportunity to visit Sherborne. While I am of course biased I can assure you that it has a special atmosphere – and there is still after 400 years a definite feel of Ralegh's presence.

John Wingfield Digby

Acknowledgements

I must first thank Dr Roger Highfield, Emeritus Fellow of Merton College, Oxford who has generously overseen my efforts to write this and two previous history books. His guidance and encouragement have spurred me on and enabled me to avoid many errors. Those which remain can be put down to me.

I would also like to thank Mr Robert Peberdy of the Victoria County History for Oxfordshire for his tireless support, suggestions and advice about writing history over several years

In researching the book I have had welcome assistance from the British Library, the National Maritime Museum, the National Archives, the Science Museum Library, the College of Arms (particularly Mr Robert Yorke their Archivist), the Royal Geographical Society (particularly Mr Francis Herbert and Mt David McNeill), the Sherborne Castle Archivist (Mrs Ann Smith), the National Trust (particularly Mrs Josephine Oxley at Petworth House) and the Honourable Society of the Middle Temple (particularly their Archivist Mrs Lesley Whitelaw). Where permission to reproduce graphics has generously been given full details are set out in the Picture Credits on p. 167.

Next I must thank Mr John Wingfield Digby for his general encouragement and support for this book, for agreeing to write the Foreword and for permitting the reproduction of pictures held at Sherborne Castle. (Full details are given in the Picture Credits on p. 167) The two pictures on the back cover may help to clarify what is not widely appreciated – that Sherborne Castle to-day has as its nucleus Ralegh's house "Sherborne Lodge" designed and built by him in the 1590s., with four wings added (in the same style) around 1617 by Sir John Digby. The "Old Castle" still stands to the north of the lake, though in a ruined state, having been "slighted" by Cromwell's forces in the Civil War.

Finally, I must acknowledge and express my thanks for the liberality of the London Fishmongers' Company which has made a substantial contribution to the costs of producing this book. The Sanderson family provided members of the Company over several generations and our William Sanderson was, for a number of years, a member of their Court

Introduction

Queen Elizabeth died on 24th March 1603. Within three days, riding with relays of horses, Sir Robert Carey brought the news to Holyrood House in Edinburgh. King James set out South at a leisurely pace to claim the English succession.[1]

Managing the succession had had two interlinked parts – the succession to the throne itself and settling who should rule under James I. Cecil handled both issues with skill and ruthlessness, but not everyone in power and favour under Elizabeth came out of it successfully. The character assassination of Ralegh by Robert Cecil and Lord Henry Howard (later Lord Northampton) successfully turned James against him, and his own behaviour, and his aggressive remarks (if John Evelyn's story is to be believed), on meeting the King early in May, ensured that his adverse opinion of Ralegh was confirmed. Action soon followed.

Almost immediately Ralegh was replaced as Captain of the Royal Guard by a Scotsman: he was, however, compensated. Next the King called in for scrutiny all the monopolies (and similar privileges – Ralegh's right to licence wine importers and retailers) granted by Elizabeth, removing over half his income, some £5,000 p.a. On 31st. May James gave orders to have Ralegh turned out of Durham House, the mansion fronting the Thames which he had occupied for 20 years by favour of the Queen. In mid-June Ralegh was questioned by the Council and by the 20th of that month he was in the Tower under suspicion of treason. Intensive investigations were initiated (into the "Bye" and "Main" plots) and, as a result Ralegh was set to stand trial for treason on 17th November, at Winchester, chosen because of an outbreak of plague in London

On 10th November Ralegh set out for Winchester in his own travelling coach, under close arrest accompanied by his gaolers – Sir William Waad, the Clerk to the Privy Council (and afterwards Lieutenant Governor of the Tower) and Sir Robert Mansell – and escorted by a troop of light horse.[2] Passing through the City the crowds were apparently hostile – shouting

Durham House, on the left: Ralegh's grace and favour London mansion

abuse and throwing missiles: Ralegh showed his disdain by ignoring them and smoking his pipe.

When the party reached the open expanse of Hounslow Heath (it seems that they followed the old Basingstoke road, approximately the A30 in modern terms) a group of mounted gentlemen who had ridden out of London to pay their respects to Ralegh and to demonstrate their support were waiting. The identity of only two of these gentlemen is known to us – William Sanderson, who had married Ralegh's niece (Margaret Snedall) and one of Sanderson's sons, also named William (then aged 16 or 17). Ralegh recognised the group and had the coach pulled up; he then addressed his kinsman:-

"Nephew Sanderson, upon my soul, I am more grieved for my engagements and debts to you, than for any other sufferings that may befall me. And good Mr. Lieutenant (of the Tower, sitting beside him) what ere becomes of me and mine, I beseech the King to be good to this worthy Gentleman: Both of them weeping, upon my oath that was present".[3]

The "engagements and debts" were a fall-out from the professional collaboration between Raleigh and Sanderson, which had started following

Sanderson's marriage to Raleigh's niece in 1584. First, the two men quickly became close friends. This, in turn, led soon after to Sanderson becoming "money-box" or private banker to Ralegh: a natural development if one considers their respective positions – Sanderson the successful merchant who had recently inherited his family fortune and Ralegh the penniless but well-connected adventurer from the West Country who had attracted the Queen's attention and a stream of royal perquisites, but whose cashflow had not yet caught up with his meteoric rise and expensive tastes. As Ralegh's ambitions rapidly expanded, the relationship adapted to match – Sanderson took a broader role as man of business/treasurer/banker.[4] These professional services continued for some ten years, covering Ralegh's ascendancy and also his setback in royal favour in 1592, following his affair with Bess Throckmorton and their secret marriage. The mutual trust between principal and treasurer, however, collapsed in 1595, leaving the "engagements and debts" owed to Sanderson – some £2,000 originally. Sanderson had borrowed about 75% of that sum (on his own credit) so that interest would have run on and penalties become payable as the stipulated repayment date had passed. In this way the total payable by Sanderson to his lender would have continued to mount up. By the time of the 1603 meeting it is clear that Ralegh still owes Sanderson money but – as we do not know whether Sanderson had settled with his lender and, if so, when he had done so – we do not know how much. It appears that the total was at least double the sum originally borrowed. The exact amount would depend on exactly when Sanderson had settled with his lender. Clearly, as Raleigh acknowledged on Hounslow Heath, he had still not reimbursed his nephew-in-law by 1603, and by then James I had started to strip him of his wealth, reducing his ability to do so. But, notwithstanding the financial arrears, Sanderson, with his son and friends, had ridden 15 miles out of London to show their respect and support.

In this way Sanderson's net worth had been depleted, by the actions of his uncle-in-law, by the equivalent of around £500,000 in to-day's money.

The quarrel in 1595 put an end to Sanderson's role as Ralegh's man of business or treasurer. (Since Ralegh never paid him a penny for his time and trouble over some ten or eleven years, a more appropriate job description would be "Honorary Treasurer".) However, despite the break, the two families maintained cordial social contacts; and some commercial connection was preserved, for example, Sanderson continued to represent Ralegh in the negotiations to apportion the treasure from the capture of the Madre de Dios in 1592.[5] The Sandersons visited Ralegh en famille regularly during his time in the Tower and their last visit was to the Gatehouse prison on the night before his execution in 1618; so the overall relationship between the two men lasted altogether around 34 years. Sanderson lived on a further 20 years, dying in 1638 at the age of 90. There seemed also to be some friendship between the two wives – Bess Raleigh (nee Throckmorton) and Margaret Sanderson (nee Snedall) – since the Sandersons entertained the newly married Raleghs, both in London and at their country house in Essex, despite their disgrace and dismissal from Court over their affair and secret marriage behind the Queen's back.[6] It is quite possible that it was these ladies who took the lead in ensuring that social intercourse between the families should continue despite the business falling-out between the two husbands.[7]

This book describes and seeks to explain the roller-coaster relationship between Ralegh and Sanderson. At the same time it locates the two men at the centre of the "Imperial Vision" – the crusade led and promoted by Ralegh and Richard Hakluyt to glorify Queen Elizabeth and England by founding an Empire, based on sea power, to replace or rival the Spanish/Portugues Empire, following the failure of the Armada. By way of practical support for this imperial crusade Ralegh and Hakluyt also conducted a campaign to improve English navigational practices, instruments and charts, which were well below European standards. This was done in two ways (i) by bringing together naval commanders with intellectuals and academics specialising in astronomy, mathematics, cartography &c. and (ii) by finding skilled artisans to make improved charts, globes and instruments. The activities of Ralegh and Sanderson, some carried on jointly, others separately, exemplify both the general thrust of the Vision, for example, Roanoke, Munster and the Manao/El Dorado expedition, and the drive to raise navigational knowledge and standards, for example, John Davis' NW Passage exploration and the Molyneux globes.

The main characters in this narrative are Ralegh and Sanderson, to whom must be added the polymath Thomas Harriot, who had joined Ralegh's household in around 1583–4 and became, effectively, his "chief of staff". The supporting cast is large and varied, ranging from Queen Elizabeth, James I, his Danish queen Anne, their eldest son Prince Henry, through Lord Burghley, Lord Salisbury, Dr John Dee, Richard Hakluyt, a large group of mathematicians/cartographers/navigators to two members of Raleigh's household of doubtful reputation – John Meere, his steward at Sherborne, and John Shelbury, his solicitor. Meere was a thoroughly bad lot, with convictions for coin cutting and violence, and was a skilful forger – he could reproduce Ralegh's signature convincingly; Shelbury was solicitor to Ralegh and later to Bess. Sanderson had occasion to accuse him, in the 1611 litigation, of arranging a forged endorsement on a deed (the actual forger was said to be John Meere) and of altering Court documents: Shelbury was accused again later, in 1626, of arranging a forged letter to assist a claim being made by Bess Ralegh herself against a prominent

London jeweller, who had advanced money to Ralegh on the security of Bess' jewellery.

Since much of the information and evidence concerning key issues in the Ralegh-Sanderson relationship is inconclusive or conflicting, it is essential that to have available convincing "portraits" or "characters" for the three principal actors – in this way we can form sensible judgments on doubtful issues based on "the balance of probabilities" and the "character" of the witness.

Ralegh's life and character have been extensively examined. While admiring Raleigh's many positive and attractive qualities we will have to consider some of the flaws – in particular the aspects most emphasised by his contemporaries – his intolerable pride and his lifelong pursuit of material gain for himself and his sons, without too much regard for the feelings and interests of others – or for the truth. Following Ralegh's death in 1618 his widow Bess initiated a campaign to upgrade or restore (depending on one's point of view) Ralegh's reputation. This process of revision has effectively continued ever since, with successive writers offering varying interpretations. However, in considering Ralegh's relationship with Sanderson, based on kinship by marriage as well as collaboration in commercial and financial affairs, he must be judged by his contemporary conduct and repute – and it must be admitted that Ralegh managed to alienate many, probably the majority, of those who knew him.

Harriot has an imposing biography based on 35 years of study by Dr. Shirley[8] and his brilliant achievements (in astronomy, mathematics, applied science and other fields) continue to receive attention from historians, including the group of scholars self-styled "Harrioteers". Harriot emerges as a man of complete integrity, unambitious, with a single-minded interest in science and knowledge, in the terms of his Epitaph "Veritatis indagator studiosissimus" (A most zealous seeker of the truth) In quoting Harriott's 1605 letter to the Privy Council, in which he sought release from imprisonment under suspicion of implication in the Gunpowder Plot, Dr Shirley

Thomas Harriot

endorses Harriott's own description of himself, commenting "to the modern reader, it seems very revealing of the character and nature of its author".[9]

> "Right honorable my very good Lordes:
> The present misry I feel being truly innocent in hart and thought presseth me to be an humble sutor to your lordships for favourable respect. All that know me can witness that I was always of honest conversation and life. I was never any busy medler in matters of state, I was never ambitious for preferments. But contented with a private life for the love of learning, that I may study freely. Wherein my labours and endeavours, if I may speak it without presumption, have been paynfull and great. And I hoped and do yet hope by the grace of god and your Lordships favour that the effects shall show themselves shortly, to the good liking & allowance of the state and common weale." (Harriot then goes on to describe the medical symptoms which he is suffering in gaol, which probably mark the start of the cancer which eventually killed him) "Therefore the innocency of my hart feeling this misery of close imprisonment with sickmess and many wantes, beside the desire of proceeding in my studies, make me a humble sutor to your honors for liberty in what measure your wisedomes shall think fit. So I shall with faithful acknowledgment spend the rest of my time so, that your honours shall not think any lawfull favour ill bestowed" In his intellectual and practical achievements Harriot proved as good as his word.

Sanderson alone has been comparatively neglected. In modern times he has been treated in his own right only in the well-known article by Dr Ruth McIntyre in 1956[10] and in the 2004 ODNB (he did not feature in the old DNB): apart from this he has figured merely as a walk-on actor in the lives of Raleigh and of Harriot. Even in Ruth McIntyre's article, which was very far-ranging, Sanderson was considered primarily as a provider of finance for English overseas exploration and settlement towards the end of the 16th century – here our immediate concern is with what sort of man he was; what contribution he made (as Honorary Treasurer) in the first 10 or 11 years of his relationship with Raleigh, and whether he was an innocent victim or a clever fraudster. The financial/legal dispute between Ralegh and Sanderson was also carefully examined in an article by Dr John Shirley in 1949–50[11] but, tantalisingly, he handed over to the reader the task of considering the evidence and delivering judgment: we will deal further with this in due course.[12]

In short, when there are conflicts of evidence, or lack of it, do we go along with Ralegh, the charismatic but arrogant and ruthless courtier, with

Sanderson the prosperous, meticulous merchant or with Harriot, the unworldly, unselfish polymath, devoted to his wide-ranging interests in mathematics, astronomy, science, linguistics, as well as in practical matters like surveying, accounting and ship-building?

As noted above, Ralegh and Harriot have been "accounted for". Part I of this book will therefore trace Sanderson's background and life leading up to his meeting with Raleigh in 1584 or 1585, and will then, in Part II, follow their relationship. The treatment will in general be chronological but where topics are self-contained (and particularly where they concern Sanderson alone) they will be dealt with at one pass.

Ralegh's recent biographer, Raleigh Trevelyan, concludes,[13] "His behaviour towards Sanderson is worrying and not fully explained". This book attempts to provide an explanation.

Part One
Worshipful Citizen and Fishmonger

Polonius	Do you know me, my lord?
Hamlet:	You are a fishmonger
Polonius	Not I, my lord
Hamlet:	Then I would you were so honest a man

Hamlet II.ii.173

The main sources for Sanderson's life are

(i) biographical notes written in 1656 by his son William, forming part of a pamphlet referred to in this book as "An Answer".[1] We will hereafter, in the interests of clarity, refer to William junior as "Sir William" – although he was only knighted late in life at the Restoration by Charles II

(ii) a "Memorandum by a Freind" written probably in or around 1626 and usually attributed to Sir William as well.

(iii) Sanderson's Address to the Gentle Reader written, apparently, by himself, and with a latin version produced by his friend, the historian William Camden, printed on the Molyneux terrestrial globes

Sanderson died in 1638 at the age of 90. The biographical note in "An Answer" was thus written nearly 20 years after Sanderson's death and over 100 years after his birth. Apart from lapse of time, we must take account of the circumstances: Sir William wrote this account in defence of himself, his wife and his father in a pamphlet battle which he was conducting with Carew Raleigh, Sir Walter's surviving son, or with some other person to whom, it is usually accepted, Carew Raleigh was supplying ammunition. The scurrilous pamphlet which Sir William was seeking to rebut, published anonymously earlier in 1656, will be referred to as "Observations"[2].

It will therefore be necessary to consider carefully[3] the value of Sir William's account – can we rely on it at all or must it be qualified on grounds either of lapse of time or of bias? The two documents (An Answer and A Memoir by a Freind) are broadly in agreement, this in itself leading to the suggestion that the Memoir also came from Sir William's hand, though at an earlier date.

Other information on Sanderson comes from various public records, particularly the court documents in the litigation between Raleigh and Sanderson 1611–13[4] and the archives of the Fishmongers' Company; and further detail on Sanderson's family has been extracted from a number of Sanderson wills, not previously published, and from a pedigree produced c.1621 and held by the College of Heralds[5].

Modern published work dealing with Sanderson includes the articles mentioned above by Dr Ruth McIntyre and Dr John Shirley; the 2004 biography of Bess Ralegh by Anna Beer, the 2002 biography of Raleigh by Raleigh Trevelyan; the 2004 article in the ODNB by Dr Anita McConnell; and a paper "Thomas Harriot and the Guiana Voyage in 1595" published in 1997 by Rosalind Davies.

1

A Younger Son

William Sanderson was probably born in 1548 – based on a definite death date in 1638 and the tradition that he lived to the age of 90. He was thus 3–4 years senior to Ralegh (his uncle by marriage) who was born in or around 1552. The explanation is that Ralegh's father married three times; Margaret Snedall's mother was a daughter by the second marriage, while Ralegh was the youngest of three children by the third marriage.

Both men were younger sons who had to make their own way in the world, but here the similarities end. Although penniless as a young man, Ralegh was socially well-connected in the West Country and it was natural for him to seek fame and wealth in the profession of arms, in which he at once displayed courage, boldness and leadership qualities. With the addition of a fine intellect, an enquiring mind, physical presence and outstanding communication skills, he was bound to attract the attention of the Queen when he found his way to Court, but his facility for making enemies, his inability to act as a team player, his poor judgment and his unwavering hatred of Spain, barred him from political advancement. The Queen was obviously fascinated by Ralegh but retained her political judgment.

Sanderson was born into a prosperous City of London family of merchants, who had been established in the City for three generations, with origins in the north east of England. Like some other Sandersons belonging to different branches of the family[1] they traced descent from Lord Bedic "alias Sanderson" established in Washington, Co.Durham around 1333[2].

The sources of the family wealth were trading in the City of London and advantageous marriages; both Sanderson's father (also confusingly, William) and his paternal grandfather (Stephen) married the heiresses of City families. By the time that Sanderson became head of his branch of the family, on the death of his elder brother in 1577, there was a property portfolio in London and southern England producing an annual income of some £700 p.a.

(around £100,000 to-day, but probably "more valuable" in what that income could purchase in terms of goods and services) We will look later at the type of trade in which Sanderson and his forebears were engaged.

The prosperity of the Sandersons was reflected in their longevity and the size of their families (and of their houses) Sanderson's father died aged 86, Sanderson himself lived to the age of 90, as did Sir William, who died in 1676. Sanderson and his siblings numbered seven, while Sanderson himself fathered eight, possibly nine children.

Sanderson had four brothers and two sisters, but it is difficult to rank them by seniority with any precision:[3] for present purposes the key point is that on the death of Sanderson's father (also William) in 1570 Sanderson's elder brother (Stephen) succeeded to the family fortune, and when he died young in 1577 Sanderson (then aged about 29) succeeded Stephen.

The Sandersons were connected with the Fishmongers' Company, one of the largest and richest of the London livery companies. Sanderson's grandfather (Stephen) and his uncle John had been members, and in his generation Sanderson himself and his elder brother Stephen; and their sister Magdalen married a "John Archer, Merchant" who was probably the Fishmonger of that name at that time. One of Sanderson's seven sons, Anthony, became a Fishmonger in 1626 by patrimony, that is, by being "presented" to the company by his father at the age of 21. John Janes, son of Sanderson's sister Alice, was also a Fishmonger. There is no positive evidence that Sanderson's father (1484–1570) was also a Fishmonger, as the Company's records prior to 1592 have been lost. He was described as a merchant in the pedigree drawn by the College of Heralds[4], but it seems likely that he was indeed a member of the Company, since there was a Sanderson mentioned as a freeman in 1537 i.e about the appropriate date.[5] In the absence of the Company's earlier records we also do not know when Sanderson himself became a Fishmonger, or whether it was by apprenticeship, patrimony or redemption i.e. by paying a fee. While apprenticeship was by far the most common mode of entry to the livery companies, as Sanderson had been working abroad, and returned after Stephen's death in 1577 to take up the family fortunes, entry by redemption around the age of 30 would be a distinct possibility – as a way for him to "replace" his deceased brother Stephen in that generation of the family.

Sanderson himself was never engaged in the fish trade, but it seems likely that one or more of his forebears had been. This supposition is supported by the fact that the family lived in the Fishmongers' "heartland", close to the Fishmongers' Hall(s)[6] and close to the main City fish market which was held in Fish Street, to-day called Bridge Street.[7] It was customary, and in some livery companies compulsory, for members to live and work in an identified area

By the middle of the 16th century it was already common for London apprentices to join a livery company without intending to follow its trade. Membership of a company via apprenticeship, the normal mode of entry, provided commercial training and an introduction to the City "network" and was the only way to become "a Citizen of London". It also qualified them to buy land in the City and might serve as a launching pad into something else, often international trade, where the long-term prospects were becoming more promising. Alternatively, a young man apprenticed to the Company's trade might, as a "career move", before finishing his apprenticeship, switch to a new master engaged in a different trade, possibly international commerce; this was known as a "turnover". This mobility affected the Fishmongers, even though the fish trade continued to flourish: with other Companies their trades declined or disappeared altogether over time, so that there was pressure to take up different employment, rather than a free choice to be made. Where it was a matter of choice, it appears that it was the livelier apprentices who were steered towards international trade as their potential was recognised in a process of "talent spotting" within the livery companies.

The location of the Sandersons' family house cannot be exactly established. It seems likely that Stephen, as the eldest son, took over the family home on his father's death, particularly as their mother re-married one George Killingworth, who seems to have lived in Kent[8] When Stephen died, Sanderson moved back to London and there is a description of his house, quoted below. It seems clear that it was not the house in which Stephen and his family had been living since Stephen left the lease of that house to his widow. Sanderson's new house was described as part of the family property portfolio – probably it had been let to a tenant. It is possible that the family's London home – in which Sanderson, Stephen and the others had been brought up – was next door to the house in which Sanderson settled when he returned to England, since it seems that the family owned two or three adjoining houses in Thames Street.[9]

Nothing is known of Sanderson's early education, but it may be safely assumed that it was thorough and successful, first, because there were many good public and private schools in the City, supervised by the Bishop of London; secondly, because high standards of reading, writing and figuring were required from budding apprentices and trainee factors,[10] and thirdly, because of his intelligent interest later in navigation and cartography, exploration and overseas settlement, mining and metallurgy and economic theory. Sanderson regretted his lack of formal higher education and hankered after men of learning, both humanistic and scientific. In An Answer Sir William explains, "He would complain of his deficiency, but was highly affected to Learned men and Arts;[In this context "arts" means applied science] witness his own words, which so pleased Camden, the famous Schollar, and his friend, that he put them into Latin...They are fully exprest and graven upon the English great Globes" This is Sanderson's "Address to the Gentle Reader" displayed on the surviving Molyneux terrestrial Globes:-

WILLIAM SANDERSON
TO THE GENTLE READER

Not in the lappe of learned skill, I ever was upbrought
Nor in the study of the stares, (with griffe I graunt) was taught
Yet while on this side arts, on that side virtue's honor
My mind admiring viewd, & rested oft upon her
Loo at my charge thou seest the evere whirling Sphere
The endless reaches of the land, and sea in sight appear.

For countries good, for worlds behoofe, for learning furtherance
Wherby our virtios englishmen their actions may advance
To visit foraine landes, where farthest coastes do lye
I have these worldes thus formd; and to worldes good apply
With word I pray you favour them, & further them with will
That arts and vertue may be deckt, with their due honor still
But yf that any better have, let them the better shewe
For learnings sake, I will not spare the charges to bestowe

Sanderson's patriotic leanings should also be noted. After naming his first son Ralegh for his wife's family he named the next two Drake and Cavendish after the circumnavigators. All his merchant banking projects had patriotic objectives; and his presentation to the Queen of the first Molyneux globes was the finale of the "grand opera" composed and orchestrated by Ralegh and Richard Hakluyt to invite the Queen and England to assume world domination based on seapower, following the failure of the Spanish/Portuguese Armada.

Further, it seems very likely that Sanderson's envy of men who had enjoyed higher education was one of the factors which attracted him to his uncle-in-law Ralegh. Despite his less attractive qualities, much commented on by his contemporaries, there was no doubt as to Ralegh's fine intellect, his wide range of interests, his skill in exposition both verbal and written – derived from or developed by his time at Oxford – as well as his charm and his phenomenal success at Court.

2

Merchant Beyond the Seas

Whether or not Sanderson was apprenticed to the Fishmongers' Company in his teens[1] he was certainly employed, as an apprentice or trainee factor, by a senior merchant Thomas Allen. This would have been, as was customary, around the age of 15, say in 1563. A member of the Skinners' Company (he was Master in 1590) and an assistant i.e. a member of the Court, of the Muscovy Company, Thomas Allen was "the Queen's merchant in the East parts beyond the seas" from 1561, effectively the chief purchasing officer for the Royal Navy. He died in 1591/2.[2] According to Sir William's account in An Answer Sanderson "was bred up in the City of London under tutelage of Mr. Allen, Queen Elizabeth's Merchant (one so called for her maritime affairs) the most part of his youth beyond Seas". This suggests that he started in London under Allen and then was sent abroad by him, perhaps around 17 years old. The Memoir gives more detail on the trade, "William Sanderson ... borne a gentleman, bred a Merchant Adventurer under the worshipful Thomas Allin Esquire Merchant unto Queen Elizabeth for her Marine causes; which said Sanderson was for himselfe and his said Maister in Denmark, Sweden and Poland; and in France Germany and Netherlands in Travaile and Trade there and elsewhere many years". This passage confirms what was the usual development for successful young factors − they started their own merchanting business, often while continuing as factor or agent for their "master". When he started trading on his own account, it seems likely that Sanderson drew on his elder brother, Stephen, for working capital out of the family resources, since in his will Stephen (he died young in 1577) directed Sanderson to sort out their joint operations and take what he felt was, in conscience, due to him. He also requested Sanderson to arrange for the income which, following their father's death, had been paid to their mother (who had re-married, to George Killingworth), should be safely steered, after their mother's death, first to Sanderson himself and ultimately to Stephen's own children. Clearly there was a close and trusting relationship between the two brothers, as well as commercial collaboration.

There is no positive explanation for the choice of Thomas Allen as Sanderson's master but the link may have been George Killingworth, who became stepfather to Sanderson and his siblings, marrying their mother after their father's death in 1570. He may well have been the same George Killingworth who was a senior factor to the Muscovy Company, of which Thomas Allen was an assistant.

The trade in which Thomas Allen was engaged, and to which he introduced Sanderson, was – like most English trade at that time – largely based on the export of English woollen cloth, and, in return the Northern European countries supplied timber, rope, flax, poldavies (a kind of canvas used for sailcloth), tallow, fish and linen.[3] From the interest in, and knowledge of, marine matters which Sanderson displayed later, including ownership of two or more small merchant ships, it looks as though his time in North Europe included organising voyages and freight in the North and Baltic Seas and the fitting-out and management of ships.[4]

From this brief account of Sanderson's background and early life it will appear that, while Ralegh was a product of the West Country gentry and aristocracy based on land, Sanderson came from a parallel "City aristocracy" – but the similarity is misleading.

In the 16th century "rank" was very much a fact of life. Younger sons of the aristocracy and gentry sometimes found their way to the City of London, and the families of successful men engaged in trade or agriculture might be translated into the landed aristocracy during their own lives, or perhaps in the next generation, but in general there was a definite "divide" between the two sections of society. The magnates, consciously or unconsciously, despised men in trade though were quick to make use of them – as a source of funds, for example, or as providers of investment opportunities or to train their younger sons for gainful employment – and City men, however rich and powerful in their own sphere, were never wholly at ease with landed aristocrats or courtiers. When City men wanted permission for some foreign venture or were seeking a charter for a new trading company, they needed to convince the Privy Council and there were always aristocrats or courtiers ready to lobby on their behalf with the Council – for some form of reward; this was naturally resented. An apposite example of the "Gentlemen v Players" situation arose over the appointment by the East India Company of the commander of their first fleet in 1600. The Privy Council pressed the claims of Sir Edward Michelmore, but the Company replied that they preferred to do business with men of their own kind, and presented a diplomatic "market justification" for their stance – if it was known that a "gentleman" was to be appointed to any position of authority the investors would be likely to withdraw their promised investment. The Company accordingly appointed James Lancaster, who had risen by merit, and he proved very successful.[5]

Sanderson and his son Sir William were both proud of their ancestry and of the Queen's direction that their arms should be "enhanced", following the publication, at Sanderson's expense, in 1592 of the Molyneux globes; though Sir William, who made his career as a courtier, seemed to be more sensitive about rank. When he came to describe how Ralegh and Sanderson became close friends (following his marriage to Ralegh's niece in 1584) and how from a friend Sanderson quickly became Ralegh's money-box or private banker he could not resist some waspish comments; and he pronounced, rather grandly, on a statement in Observations, that Sanderson "disdained to be his (that is, Ralegh's) servant".

The difference in "rank" seems to have been an important factor in several issues which arose between the two men in the course of their relationship.

3

Merchant to Merchant Banker

Sanderson's time as an expatriate factor and merchant lasted about 12 years. As his elder brother Stephen died in 1577 we can place his return to London in 1578 or 1579 when he was about 30 years old.[1] He thus suddenly found himself, at an early age, the head of the family and in possession of substantial investment income, in addition to his earnings as a merchant. Sir William in An Answer explains, "His elder brother dying, hee became heire to £700 per annum, land of Inheritance, in severall places viz. in London, at Layton in Essex, (being his Country house and land, of retiring) at Tunbridge in Kent, at Barstable in Devon; in Ireland, of great value, until the rebellion of Tyrone, and then sold for £1500; at Lambeth in Surrey". Of these properties, so far only his London house (see below) and the Irish landholding have been located, but Sanderson is found later buying and selling property in Surrey, Kent, Devon (and also Somerset) and Lambeth, no doubt disposing of, or adding to, the portfolio. Sir William was not quite accurate over the Irish holding. His father did not inherit it, as the account implies: he bought it as an investment in 1592 from one of the "undertakers" in the Munster Plantation and sold out in 1602.[2]

There is little direct evidence of how Sanderson spent the next five years or so after returning to live in England but from what we have an adequate account can be deduced.

The will of Sanderson's elder brother Stephen makes it clear that the two brothers had been collaborating in Sanderson's North European trading, so it seems likely that Sanderson continued this business from his new London base, replacing his brother Stephen, and sending out into the market an agent or factor to replace himself. The switch from "factor in the field" to "merchant adventurer" in London was a natural and normal one, although in Sanderson's case it was accelerated by Stephen's early death. It seems very unlikely that Sanderson would have simply abandoned the Northern

European business which he had built up over the previous 10 years or so, starting as a "trainee" under Thomas Allen. That he continued in some commercial activity (rather than "retiring" to live on the income of the family property portfolio) seems certain, since (i) he is found owning several small merchant ships which accompanied John Davis in 1585–7 on his exploration of the NW Passage and were involved in efforts to sustain the Roanoke settlement at about the same time (ii) his activities serving Government[3] are based on his being a merchant of standing.

The most likely progression is that Sanderson continued as a merchant, trading with North Europe and, as he familiarised himself with the London "investment scene" engrafted upon this activity his various investment banking projects – becoming in its earlier sense a "merchant banker". Sanderson was by nature careful and methodical and would have at this stage after ten years abroad little knowledge of the rapid developments taking place in English exploration and trade (beyond Northern Europe) and no circle of friends, contacts, potential partners and so on, so it is not surprising that it was some years before he started to invest in the 1580s and 1590s as a patron and financier of exploration, foreign trade and settlement, with strong patriotic overtones.

Apart from his commercial activities (and perhaps looking for a wife) two obvious priorities for Sanderson on returning home were to establish a London house and to inspect the family's property portfolio.

Sanderson inherited, and seems to have retained, a country house at Leyton in Essex: his son Drake appears to have been born there, since he was baptised at Leyton on 12th August 1593.[4] Sir William describes his father's new London home – it appears that it was part of the existing property portfolio, which had been let, rather than being already occupied by the family: "At his returne home, he settled himselfe in a faire house, now the Hoope Taverne in St. Magnus Parish London, his Inheritance there with other Tenements, His cote, Arms and Name, with the year of our Lord fixed in convenient places of that house doe now evidence." He is registered as paying subsidy of £10 in 1582 in St. Magnus' Parish, Bridge Ward. While it now no longer exists we can identify its approximate location. There were two Hoop taverns close by, one on the east side of Fish Street Hill which ran steeply up from the north end of London Bridge to Fish Street (now known as Bridge Street), and another in Thames Street itself.[5] Both taverns survived the Great Fire and were visited by Samuel Pepys.[6] The name "Hoop" figures frequently in tavern names, though it is rare to find a tavern simply named "The Hoop" (except by way of abbreviation); since the sign for the tavern was often hung outside in an iron hoop, and a more usual name would be "The xxxx on the Hoop". We can identify Sanderson's house as being the Hoop Tavern in Thames Street because (i) on other occasions there are references to this street as being the site of his house, and (ii) when he came to sell it in 1605 the conveyance described it as "The Dolphin in the Hoop".[7] The parish church of St. Magnus the Martyr, where Sanderson was married on 4th May 1584, at that time stood at the north end of London Bridge. The lay-out of the streets was altered when the new London Bridge was built further to the west. In Sanderson's day Gracechurch Street, then sometimes called Gracious Street, and Bridge Street, then called Fish Street, ran in a straight north-south line to the north end of old London Bridge. After the Great Fire the Monument was built on this main street: but it is now a block back from the entry to the modern London Bridge.

If Sanderson did set out to inspect the various family property holdings (as suggested above) he may well have visited Devon, travelling either overland or by sea. Although the Sanderson property there was at Barstable (Barnstaple) i.e. in the north of the county, he may have found his way to Exeter, where his future father-in-law, Hugh Snedall, was a merchant,[8] and made the acquaintance of the guild of Exeter merchants whom he enlisted in the next decade as fellow investors with himself in backing the NW Passage exploration of John Davis. He may also of course have met his future wife during a visit to Exeter.

After some twelve years overseas Sanderson was able to start on what young men commencing their careers in the City (like his brother Stephen) had been able to do from the outset – establish a network of friends, acquaintances, potential business partners and so on, which have always been the hallmark of the City of London and other commercial centres. It is to be expected, too, that others will be keen to make the acquaintance of a young man, who is already a successful merchant and who has come into a fortune at an early age: Ralegh in his "penniless" days (he first came to Court in 1580) may well have fallen into this category, when Sanderson married his niece.

We know, from Sanderson himself, that he only met Ralegh following his marriage to his niece in 1584, but it seems quite likely that a few years earlier he became acquainted with the group of young men, mainly Oxford graduates, who had joined the crusade mounted by Ralegh and Richard Haluyt (the "Imperial Vision") to stimulate foreign exploration and settlement, even though at that time he did not meet Ralegh himself. This possibility is supported by the fact that Sanderson's two main investment banking projects – backing John Davis and the Molyneux globes – were structured around several of these individuals. Ralegh started to build such a following after his time at Oxford, for example, Thomas Harriot the polymath, who joined his household around 1583–4)); Lawrence Keymis, his faithful lieutenant who committed suicide in 1618 after his disastrous

Gerard Mercator and Jodocus Hondius

attack on San Tome in Guyana, in which Wat Ralegh was killed; Robert
Hues, mathematician. and geographer, who wrote the manual for the
Molyneux globes "Tractatus de Globis" and dedicated it to Ralegh;
Edward Wright, mathematician and cartographer, who provided the
mathematical basis for Mercator's Projection and produced the 1599 World
Mappe; Richard Hakluyt, who sought out all men with interests in marine
matters and overseas trade and settlement;[9] his Gilbert half-brothers (Adrian
and Humphrey) and John Davis, originally their neighbour in Devon.
Humphrey Gilbert was probably the link with Dr. John Dee, the polymath
with a special interest in cartography, navigation and exploration, who was
consulted by Government; and Dee, in turn, had a close relationship with
Gerardus Mercator in the Low Countries; while John Davis who knew
Emery Molyneux, originally a maker of mathematical instruments before he
made the famous English globes, probably introduced him to Sanderson as
a source of finance for the globes.

From these individuals we can probably select as the main source of
inspiration or prime mover Richard Hakluyt who was essentially a

commentator and facilitator (as well as being a self-appointed economic adviser to Government) rather than a competitive participant. Ralegh inspired his "circle" with his lifelong dream – to build an English empire in America – and members of it worked on the projects which he launched to realise it and in the advertising/propaganda campaign which he orchestrated to promote it.[10]

4

A Link with Frobisher?

It is appropriate to divert at this point to consider briefly the three voyages in search of the North West Passage made by Sir Martin Frobisher in June 1576, June 1577 and May 1578, since the 2004 article on Sanderson in the ODNB[1] states that he funded these three voyages. While the sources quoted in the article do not provide support for this proposition, and there are a number of arguments against it, the author of the ODNB article, Dr Anita McConnell, has an extensive knowledge of archival sources and may well have picked up a clue which has been generally missed. Frobisher's voyages had their genesis in a meeting on 20th May 1576 at the Mortlake house of Dr John Dee, the astronomer and navigator who also practised (as did many men of science), astrology, alchemy, spiritualism and other creative arts. At the time of this meeting and indeed at the time of the first voyage's departure (7th June 1576) it seems clear that Sanderson was still an expatriate factor/merchant somewhere in North Europe, who returned only occasionally to England. As his elder brother Stephen died in September/October 1577 Sanderson would probably not have been in England at the time of despatch of the second expedition either; but it seems unlikely, anyway, that he would have invested in the first voyage when he was fully engaged in Europe. Apart from timing difficulties, a more potent argument is that Sanderson would probably have been unwilling to contemplate high risk investment like NW Passage exploration when his only wealth depended on his trading – he did not succeed to the family fortune (with an unearned income of £700 p.a.) until the end of 1577 or early 1578.[2] Like most successful merchants Sanderson was a careful and methodical man: before he got involved in the next decade with the NW Passage expeditions organised by Adrian Gilbert and commanded by John Davis he requested Henry Lane, a factor of the Mucovy Company, to produce a summary of attempts on the Northern Passages over the previous

30 years.[3] The summary's latest entry was for 1583, which suggests that Sanderson only took the decision to become involved with the Northern Passages in that year or later. Further, on personality grounds Sanderson would have hardly have been attracted by Frobisher's character – a ferocious fighting commander with really no other attractive or redeeming features who despised men of trade[4]; nor would he have welcomed the diversion of Frobisher's efforts, after the first voyage, from exploration into a spurious gold rush, involving even higher risks, which in due course realised substantial losses. Finally, on the possible connection with Frobisher, it should be noted that his latest biographer[5] makes no reference to Sanderson.

Accordingly it is suggested that Sanderson did not, after all, finance Frobisher's NW Passage exploration.

5

Other Interests for a City Man

To complete the description of Sanderson's personality and character at the time that he met Ralegh in 1584, it is convenient to collect here some of the "extra-curricular" activities in which he was engaged.

Education and "Arts"

One of Sanderson's characteristics throughout his life was his regret that, as a younger son in a City family, he never enjoyed higher education, and, perhaps for this reason, was drawn towards those who had.[1] He was clearly intelligent and – perhaps to compensate for this disappointment – pursued many intellectual and practical interests, as opportunity offered. The combination of natural abilities and Oxford polish was probably one of the characteristics which attracted Sanderson to Ralegh. Sir William in An Answer notes his father's interest in the "Arts" (which in this context meant applied science) when he describes the Molyneux Globes[2] and the demonstration of a perpetual motion machine organised by Prince Henry[3], and indeed Sanderson himself spells out his interest in the "Address to the gentle Reader" on the Molyneux terrestrial globes.[4] With his experience in the import-export trade and his repertoire of additional skills, Sanderson in the 1580s was recruited to the network of knowledgeable non-government "experts" which Lord Burghley built up;[5] justifying Sir William's claim in An Answer that his father enjoyed friendly relations with senior Government figures. The Memoir makes the same point "And in respect of his majesties office and service for him was well knowne in Court in the dayes of the Duke of Norffolke and afterwards in the time of the Lordes Burleigh and Leicester".

A Patriot

Sanderson showed marked patriotism both in his private and professional life. As mentioned above he named three sons after Ralegh, Drake and Cavendish. Of his seven sons, Sir William became a courtier and author, Cavendish a lawyer, Anthony a Fishmonger and, perhaps therefore a merchant, but the other four sought military or naval employment "beyond the seas"[6] Sanderson's activities had underlying patriotic objectives – in his collaboration with Ralegh, exploration or settlement in North and South America, and the Plantation of Munster; on his own account, the NW Passage exploration of John Davis, the Molyneux globes, commissioning an armillary sphere as a gift for Prince Henry and financing John Norden's Speculum Britannicae (county guide books and maps). His many years of pushing mercantilist ideas for trade financing (never in the event accepted or implemented) were motivated by a desire to improve the profitability of English exports, mainly woollen cloth. Sanderson's patriotism is spelled out (as is his regret over missed educational opportunities) in his dedication on the Molyneux globes.[7] Ralegh too consistently promoted the interests of England and the Queen, but for him this was always linked with his own search for power and wealth, so it is probably fair to say that if Sanderson's patriotism was less vocal than Ralegh's, it was also less selfish.

Mining and Metallurgy

Somewhere along the line Sanderson acquired knowledge of minerals and mining, probably during his early days in North Europe, since Germany and Austria were pre-eminent in these fields in the 16th century. It was from those countries that Lord Burghley attracted know-how and entrepreneurs to develop the English mining/metalworking industries under the banners of the Mines Royal and the Minerals and Battery Works Companies, originally chartered in 1568.

In 1595 Burghley employed Sanderson to analyse some of the ore brought back from South America by Ralegh's Manao/El Dorado expedition.

Around 1600 Sanderson is also found as a member of the Minerals and Battery Works Company. Later, in the first decade of the 17th century, his mining expertise enabled Sanderson to "farm" some of the properties of the Mines Royal Company, with disastrous results for him and the family fortunes.[8] He also invested in the Copper & Brass Mill.at Isleworth. This too seems to have been unsuccessful and he became involved in litigation with John Broad (Brade), a fellow-investor.[9]

Ship Management, Cartography, Navigation

Sanderson's skill in marine matters also seems to have stemmed originally from his time in North Europe where goods were moving continuously in the North and Baltic Seas. Later he acquired two or three merchant ships of his own: they were employed in the efforts to relieve the Roanoke settlement and in the NW Passage voyages of John Davis, and no doubt in the meantime traded commercially. They may have undertaken some privateering. Sanderson became knowledgeable about charts and navigation and, as a result, was able to discuss these matters on a professional basis with John Davis, an outstanding navigator, concerning his voyages seeking the NW Passage. When leaving on his first voyage to South America, early in 1595, Ralegh invited Sanderson to accompany him to Plymouth to oversee the readiness of the ships for sea. In the 1611 litigation the Ralegh team belittled Sanderson's naval credentials compared with Ralegh's: this appears to have been without justification, and indeed, though Ralegh employed ships and naval commanders, his personal achievements seem to have been military rather than naval.[10]

A Commercial Arbitration

An item from the public records in 1587, which seems not to have received much notice, throws an interesting cross light on Sanderson's standing with Government at the age of 39. On 16th February in that year the Privy Council met at Greenwich. One of the items of business was a complaint by a merchant named John Chilton against "one James Lancaster of London, merchaunte". Chilton was probably a brother of a Leonard Chilton who was an English merchant living in Andalusia, part of the "Brotherhood of St. George", an association of English expatriate merchants which operated in the area around Cadiz and Seville under the patronage of the Duke of Medina Sidonia.[11] James Lancaster was a rising merchant and ship commander, from a middle class background in North Hampshire, who joined the Skinners' Company but branched out into international trade in Portugal, Spain and the Levant: he subsequently led the First Fleet of the East India Company in 1601 and was knighted on his return in 1603. Chilton had complained that Lancaster owed him money, and to the Privy Council "it should appear that there is a good rounde somme of monie due to Chilton". The Council therefore wrote to four merchants stating that they were themselves too busy "by reason of her Majesties other services and affaires" to investigate, and requiring them "or anie three or two of you" to sort the matter out. The merchants were

Richard Staper, Sanderson, John Archer and John Wattes. John Archer was probably Sanderson's brother-in-law, a fellow member of the Fishmongers' Company[12]; he was a dealer in spices and an appraiser for the Court of Admiralty. Richard Staper was one of the leading London merchants of the day, having interests in all the overseas markets. John Watts, later knighted, was also an important merchant who was the leading backer of privateering expeditions.[13] The nature of Chilton's complaint is not for present purposes of great importance (it probably concerned some business in Spain), and Lancaster was obviously cleared of any wrongdoing, since Staper and Watts both supported him later, Staper through the East India Company, of which he was a director, and Watts with regard to Lancaster's privateering Recife Raid in 1594–5, sending his son to serve under Lancaster. What is significant is that the incident brackets Sanderson (and John Archer), in the eyes of the Privy Council, with two of the top City of London merchants, who were also high in the civic government of the City: both served as Master of the Clothworkers' Company, Staper was to become an Alderman and Watts Lord Mayor. At the same time it corroborates the claim by Sir William, in An Answer, that his father was in good standing with the Court and Government.

A Diplomatic Assignment

Two years later, in 1589, Sanderson was officially employed again, and on this occasion the Queen was directly involved. Prince Charles of Sweden wrote to Queen Elizabeth seeking her permission for him to send certain cargoes to Spain, against which England was attempting to maintain a blockade. Sanderson acted as middleman in conveying the letter from Sweden to England. There is no record of what reply was made – probably a qualified approval, depending on the exact nature of the cargo – but later Sanderson was directed to accompany William Burrow and Christopher Baker to examine two ships belonging to Prince Charles "to inform of what he knew by the conference he had with them, having also brought part of their requests and offers". We do not know the outcome but the degree of confidence in Sanderson on an assignment as much diplomatic as commercial is of interest. Sanderson was on this occasion described as "Sir Walter Raleigh's servant" – this would not have pleased Sir William.[14] It may be that on this assignment Sanderson had to report directly to the Queen: certainly Sir William claims in An Answer that he did from time to time meet and converse with her.

A Valuable Contribution to the Public Finances

There is an intriguing statement in the Memoir concerning another public service by Sanderson – which has not yet been clarified, "And also he did bring unto the Queenes Majestie in ye latter dayes of her Rayne a Present, or Project, by which the late King's Majestie hath received into his Coffers more than £100,000 sterling. And never as yet asking any one penny in recompense (for that his service done) of her nor his late majestie, nor will he ever do (as he intends) until he has done his Majestie twice better service than that was, which still continueth and bringeth unto his Majestie a yearly revenue of many thousand pounds stock" No doubt this "project" related to some aspect of English international trade, perhaps to do with the collection of customs.

Madre de Dios

In 1592 a Commission was established to apportion the enormous prize taken from this Portuguese carrack. Sanderson, described as "merchant", was appointed to speak "for Sir Walter Raleigh, and for the captains, masters, gentlemen, soldiers, mariners and fellows in the said voyage."[15]

An Early "Economist"

We may now describe another activity which Sanderson took up after he returned to London around 1578 and, indeed, maintained for a further 60 years until the end of his long life. Sir William in An Answer explains, "My father was not wanting in the commendable mysterie of the Merchant Adventurers; witnesse those long since printed Tractes, and many Manuscripts and Papers, which I have of his (and one Malynes his Assistant) for the discovery of the secret mysterie of Bullion and Monie, the exchange and rechange, single and double usance of Monie among Merchants; the Cambio Regis, of which the Treasurers, Burghley and Sackville, would say That Sanderson understood the Theory and Practick more than most English merchants. Sir Abraham Dawes did professe, that he knew Mr Sanderson a worthy Merchant; and certainly (said he) in comparison of him, many of us are but Pedlars".[16] Apart from the small inaccuracy about Gerald Malynes, it looks as though Sir William, a "court historian", was somewhat out of his depth when he describes his father's commercial interests) In short, Sanderson set himself up as one of the early "economists" or commentators on trade and economic matters, and as such, enjoyed the ear and respect of senior ministers over a very long period. Several of his works have survived (see Appendix A): the extract quoted above confirms that when Sir William was writing An Answer, in 1656, he had a number of his father's works in front of him.

On occasions these works have been attributed to Sir William, probably because – prior to the McIntyre Article in 1956 – little attention had been given to the father and son and the fact that both were named William caused them to be confused with each other. However it now seems clear that the author was Sanderson, since (i) Sir William was a courtier and an "arts man" and had no experience in trade or financial matters (ii) the published work, definitely identified as Sir William's, reflects this, being "court histories" and a history of painting ("Graphice") (iii) the quotation (above) from An Answer shows that Sir William was floundering even when simply describing his father's "tractes" on foreign exchange and trade financing. There is no reason, however, to doubt his comment that his father enjoyed the respect of Ministers for his knowledge of commerce and finance.

To put into context Sanderson's activity as an economic commentator it is necessary to range briefly over England's main export trade (of wool and woollen cloth) from around 1500 to around 1630, when the "mercantilist" policy of intervention was abandoned. Putting on one side the benefits of hindsight, what is significant for present purposes is that Sanderson for over 50 years was regarded as a credible adviser to Government on trade financing problems.

English Imports & Exports 1500–1630

A convenient summary of English imports and exports for the first half of the 16th century is given in the map on p. 23. However the commodities listed and their geographical sources are not of equal importance so some highlights may be noted:-

- the largest single ingredient in England's international trade was woollen exports, which by the mid 16th century amounted to 90% of all English exports
- before 1500 the woollen exports were mainly raw wool, but woollen cloth exports built up rapidly and by mid 16th century amounted to 90% of all woollen exports
- the next largest ingredient in English international trade (though far smaller than woollens) was the import from Northern Europe of naval materials and stores e.g. timber, oars, pitch, canvas, cordage,

Early Tudor Commerce 1500–1550

hemp. This was the market in which Sanderson was trained and in which he prospered as a merchant; and of course the market from which he developed his economic theories.[17]

- apart from naval stores most imports were "desirables" rather than "necessities" e.g. wine, spices, silk and other fine cloths
- London handled more trade than all the other English ports (known as the "outports") put together

- most of the woollen exports were sold via the entrepot of Antwerp until the 1550s
- from around 1550 English merchants made strenuous efforts (encouraged by government) to find other, more distant export markets, and chartered trading companies were established to channel and regulate this – Muscovy/Russian (1555), Spanish/Portuguese (1577), Eastland (Norway, Sweden, Lithuania, Prussia and the Baltic Sea) (1579), Turkey/Levant (1581), Venice (1583), Barbary (North Africa) (1585), Africa (1588), Second Levant (1592), East India (1600)
- Antwerp was closed to English exporters in the 1550s
- England's launch into general international trade was based on the marketability of English wool and woollen cloth, allied with the determination of the leading London merchants to import oriental spices from their sources, rather than buying them from European or Levantine middlemen.

Since mediaeval times England had produced and exported high quality raw wool, supplying the large weaving industries in the Low Countries and North Italy. The success of this trade led to (i) "enclosures" i.e. turning over additional English land to sheep runs, which caused social upheaval and unemployment (ii) the realisation that added value could be obtained by exporting not wool but finished or part-finished cloth, preferably the former. Sheep breeders, master weavers and cloth merchants realised enormous fortunes; but the risks resulting from the widespread dependency on wool seem not to have been considered until problems arose. However customer resistance built up in the course of the 16th century, with the quality of European weaving, finishing, dying &c. becoming equal or superior to the English, and often cheaper too. In addition, alternative sources of good quality wool were developed e.g. Spain.[18] The European customers would therefore have preferred to buy wool or part-finished cloth, but complicated, interlocking restrictive practices within the English wool trade,[19] combined with a difficulty in coming to terms with the fact that their previously dominant position had disappeared, seem to have prevented the exporters from making the appropriate flexible responses.[20] Export volumes and revenue suffered, followed by unemployment and insolvencies in the English trade.

The woollen export trade also suffered from non-commercial problems. Over the 16th century there was a series of inflationary and deflationary periods, each giving problems to exporters, for whom ideal conditions are stable currency rates over a long period. The major influence was probably the debasement and subsequent restoration of the English currency – the

English silver currency was debased in 1526 and 1543 (by Henry VIII) and in 1548 and 1551 (by Edward VI). When the damaging effects of inflation were recognised Queen Elizabeth, on the advice of Sir Thomas Gresham, the leading London merchant and the Crown Agent managing the national debt by borrowing in Europe, resolved to restore the purity of the currency: this was commenced in 1552.

There were a number of other events or developments which had a tendency to encourage either inflation or deflation, but historians are not agreed on exactly what they were or on their comparative weighting. For example, inflation is thought to have been encouraged by rising population, bad weather and poor harvests, gold and silver being released from religious houses or imported from the Americas or mined in Germany; deflation, on the other hand, by falling population resulting from a run of poor harvests and plague.

The "authorities" from the Privy Council downwards were sensitive to the troubles of the woollen export industry but no effective measures were taken, except the restoration of the purity of the currency. The exporting merchants themselves, when times were hard, tended to take the steps normally available to large scale operators – (i) they downgraded the quality and thus reduced the cost of the merchandise, producing lighter cloths.[21] (ii) they simply reduced the scale of their operations, or (iii) they diversified, for example, Sir Thomas Gresham made a killing for his family company in 1548–9 by exporting English tin to Europe where market-rigging had enhanced the prices.[22] While the big men earned lower profits, but survived, the real distress was felt amongst employees and the self-employed operators.

Sanderson and his fellow economic commentators, particularly Gerald Malynes, around the end of the 16th century, floated the idea that the woollen cloth exporters were suffering from "unfavourable exchange". This description applied primarily to the exchange rates between sterling and the European currencies but seems also to have embraced the availability and cost of credit, in particular the cost of using bills of exchange, which the exporters needed. The remedy recommended by Sanderson and Malynes for this real or perceived problem was to establish state officials (the "Official Exchanger") who would have the monopoly of handling such transactions at "official rates".[23] These recommendations were promoted (and also keenly contested) over some 30 years from around 1600 but were, in the event, never implemented; which suggests that, first, that the analysis was mistaken and, secondly, that the authorities were not convinced that the recommended remedy would be effective. With hindsight it looks as though the "unfavourable exchange" was not the problem as such, but rather an evaluation by the market-place of the waning attraction of English woollen exports over a long period. With woollen cloth forming around 80% of all English exports, it is not difficult to see lack of enthusiasm for products which were less competitive than in times past spilling over into a lack of enthusiasm for English currency. The experience of two World Wars in the 20th century demonstrates that exchange control, with fixed "official rates", can work, at least for a period, but only if it is rigidly enforced on all currency transactions. Once free or "black" markets are permitted to develop market forces regain control.[24]

International trade tends to involve, between exporter and the ultimate customer, differences in time, geographical distance and currencies; and the bill of exchange was developed to bridge these differences. A cost to the exporter was involved, when he discounted his bill, so this seems to have been the reason why the "unfavourable exchange" accusation was levelled at the cost of credit as well as the currency exchange rates. The traditional view of credit as "usury"[25] might also have been an influence, on the basis that an Official Exchanger might regulate the cost of obtaining credit by using a bill of exchange.[26]

The progression in religious, moral and legal attitudes to "usury" i.e. lending, over the 16th century was remarkable.[27] At the outset the religious/moral view, based on the Old and New Testaments and the opinions of the Early Church was stern and uncompromising – "usury" covered all lending and credit arrangements where, under the terms of the original agreement, the lender recovered any benefit in excess of the capital sum originally lent; and such arrangements were forbidden and illegal. Within about 30 years, by around 1600, "usury" had effectively abandoned its traditional all-embracing scope and assumed its modern meaning – lending on extortionate or unconscionable terms. Sanderson seems to have maintained the extreme, traditional, religious view that all lending at interest is wrong, while Malynes moved with the times and condemned only what was called "biting usury" i.e. extortionate terms for lending.

In their books and pamphlets, and their submissions to Parliament and the official committees considering the trade financing problems, Malynes and Sanderson maintained their views on "unfavourable exchange" and the need to have fixed official rates set and operated by public officials for some 30 years, but never persuaded the authorities to adopt them.[28] The opposite, more "modern" view, enunciated mainly by two other "economists" Edward Misselden and Thomas Mun prevailed, that exchange rates perceived as "unfavourable" were not themselves the problem, but were merely the measure of the unsatisfactory "balance of trade" with regard to English exported woollens. Misselden was, like Sanderson, an independent commentator but Mun was a highly respected senior employee and spokesman for the East India Company; he was particularly concerned to defend the EIC practice of exporting cash to prime their trading pump. The school of Sanderson and Malynes regarded the export of "bullion" or "specie" as harmful to England per se, even though the objective (and usually the actual result) was that goods of a higher value would eventually return to England. Later the EIC came to realise that the most valuable medium of exchange in southern Asia was not cash but high quality Gujerati cottons.

Malynes and Sanderson were later labelled "mercantilists". This description was applied to individuals who in the 16th and 17th centuries advocated certain objectives or measures designed to improve a country's financial health or its net worth, such measures to be taken through direct official intervention. These objectives were:-

- increase in exports and reduction in imports
- prohibition of the export of bullion and coin
- at a later date, restricting colonial territories from trading except with the mother country and from transporting goods except in vessels of the mother country.

Apart from the hoped-for result – improvement in the national economy, and the modus operandi – direct government intervention, the description "mercantilist" is thus somewhat imprecise. The most active "interventionist" of the period was probably William Cecil, Lord Burghley, both with his own ideas and his backing of other people's, but scholars are not unanimous in dubbing him "mercantilist".

While Sanderson's views did not prevail, they certainly received national attention over many years, and it seems clear that he and his ally Malynes were widely respected as knowledgeable on international trade matters. It is noteworthy that in 1622 Sanderson, at the age of 74 and newly released after eight or nine years in debtors' prisons, was immediately appointed, with Malynes and some other respected individuals, to the Committee on trade problems set up by James I.[29] Even later Sanderson continued to bombard the Crown, by then Charles I, with papers advocating Royal Exchangers to manage currency exchange transactions and control "usury".[30]

Royal Connections

Sanderson entertained the Queen twice in 1692 at his house at Newington Butts in Surrey, 1½ miles south of London Bridge, when he presented her on the first occasion with a terrestrial, and on the second a celestial, globe built by Emmery Molyneux. Sanderson had provided the money (over £1000) to finance the project, which is described more fully below at p. 58ff. Sir William in An Answer suggests a closer acquaintance with the Queen though he may have been mistaken, "[Sanderson] was instructed soly, to negotiate at Court, concerning the Queen's part in all the Spanish goods. In which he was made Commissioner and thereby to attend the then Lord Treasurer Burghley and often times to speake with the Queen, by favour of such as had relation to Her." It seems clear that this reference is to the allocation by a Commission of prize money from the Madre de Dios, the rich Portuguese carrack captured in 1592. However, Sanderson was not a Commissioner but the representative of Sir Walter Ralegh and the officers and men engaged in the action. This error by Sir William (which seems to be repeated in the Memoir by a Freind) does not necessarily mean that his father did not from time to time converse with the Queen, and indeed it seems unlikely that she would have visited Sanderson's home over the globes[31] if he was not already known to her. The argument for a long-standing and closer relationship is bolstered by the elaborate and extravagant imagery of the globes; the witty comments made by the Queen on the two occasions when Sanderson presented the terrestrial and celestial globes to her at his home, and by the Queen's order that Sanderson should have his arms embellished by the Heralds, with a "Globe Terrestriall, affixed to the Sun in lustre, proper" replacing the Talbot as crest, and a new motto "Opera Mundi" in place of "Rien sans Dieu". The inscription on the globe, composed by Sanderson and rendered into latin by the historian William Camden, invites the Queen and England to assume the domination of the world, relying on sea power.

Sanderson's role in the attempt by Prince of Sweden to obtain Queen Elizabeth's permission to trade with Spain, despite the English blockade, (described above at p. 20) may also have involved one or more audiences with the Queen.

When James I succeeded Queen Elizabeth in 1603 we have seen that he moved rapidly to strip Ralegh of his royal perquisites and organise his prosecution for treason. After a cruel charade on the scaffold commuting a traitor's death to indefinite imprisonment in the Tower, Ralegh spent thirteen years there. During this period he cultivated James's Danish Queen Anne and their eldest son Prince Henry. While there is no positive evidence that Prince Henry ever met Ralegh[32] his admiration of him and efforts to persuade his father to release him, thwarted by Henry's early death aged 18 in 1612, suggests that he probably did. It is interesting to find that Sanderson (together, it must be said, with a number of other prominent men) also "made up to" the royal heir who was something of a prodigy, learned, athletic, charismatic, a contrast to his father.[33] This move is unlikely to have been made before 1604 when Prince Henry was ten years old. Sir William tells the story in An Answer, "He employed Wright and other mathematicians, to compose and frame, that then admired double Sphear, presented by Sanderson to Prince Henry, with a manuscript of the use thereof; not long since remaining in the Library of St. James". The "double sphere" was an armillary sphere − a three dimensional representation of the earth and the heavenly bodies, having the earth as a small metal sphere in the centre surrounded by a metal lattice-work larger sphere on which the heavenly bodies were mounted. Sanderson was known to Edward Wright, the mathematician, who was a tutor to Prince Henry. Wright certainly produced an armillary sphere and published a guide to its use, "Description and Use of the Sphere".[34] The manual was published in 1613 i.e. after Prince Henry's death in 1612, so presentation of the guide to the Prince *in MS form* would fit with Sir William's account. Prince Henry responded to Sanderson's present,. "He, knowing my father's affection to Arts, commended Bloys, a man of skill pretending to the perpetual motion, which was endeavoured at my father's house then at Islington, and brought to excellent observation, and at his cost and charges. A mighty Wheel it was, of large circumference, erected upon beams, with massy bolts of iron….which at the first motion was of that might and swiftness, as, with horrour and noise of clattering the bolts, affrighted the Prince and company, the first that saw its motion…." Given the extensive, dramatic description (only a small part is quoted here) perhaps Sir William was present: in 1604 he was around 22 years old.

Was Sanderson seeking the patronage of the Prince quite independently, or was he perhaps aligning his efforts alongside those of his uncle-in-law, who clearly saw Queen Anne (and her Danish relations) and Prince Henry as the best advocates to regain him his freedom? It is tempting to accept the latter explanation.

The Fishmongers' Company

In the absence of surviving records, it is possible that Sanderson obtained the freedom of the Company by redemption when he retuned to London around 1578. He certainly was an Assistant i.e. a member of the Court, but here, too, we do not know when he was appointed. A date around the mid-1580s might be suggested by which time Sanderson was well established back in the City of London. He was dismissed as an Assistant, together with several others, in 1605 on the ground that he lived outside the City and did not attend to his duties. At that time he was living at Newington Butts, about 1½ miles south of London Bridge: he moved to Islington in 1606.

6

Marriage and Family

Sanderson married Margaret Snedall on 4th May 1584 at St. Magnus' Church, Thames Street, at the foot of old London Bridge. This was the Sandersons' parish church.

It was suggested above that he might have first met his bride in Exeter, where her parents lived, in the course of a commercial visit, either to Margaret's father (who was a merchant in that city) or to the Guild of Exeter merchants, with whom he certainly had dealings in the next decade, recruiting them to invest in the first two of John Davis' three NW Passage voyages.

Ralegh was perhaps a guest at the wedding. This is not clear from Sanderson's own account of their first meeting[1].

"Your said subject about thirty years since did marry and take to wife Margaret Snedall daughter of Hugh Snedall and niece of Sir Walter Raleigh, Knight, that is to say his sister's daughter, by means of which intermarriage your subject and Sir Walter Raleigh became acquainted and grew into inward love and friendship..." It looks as though Sanderson was bowled over by his uncle-in-law's charm, abilities and superior education, his meteoric rise at Court and a rapidly growing stream of Royal cash and perquisites; so that it was hardly surprising that he soon began to act as Ralegh's "money-box" or (unpaid) private banker. Sanderson's petition continues[2] "So as your said subject at the request and for the good of the said Sir Walter Raleigh and for his credit stood bound and engaged for him by bonds money disbursed and otherwise to the value of £50,000 and upwards at one instant [of] time when the credit of the said Sir Walter Raleigh of itself could not otherwise attaine thereunto". Sanderson is not here suggesting that he was unwilling to help or that he was in some way pressurised – no doubt as a careful merchant he saw sufficient cash coming in to Ralegh from the Queen's favour to protect his personal position – but he does goes on to complain about his later treatment, to which we will come in due course. The rapid transformation from nephew-in-law to close friend to unpaid private banker was noted in somewhat sarcastic terms by Sir William in An Answer, many years later, having, it would seem, his father's cash books at hand, "Sir Walter returning home to his Center the Court, his sister's daughter (Mrs Snedall) married to Sanderson, who was become the Queens Customer and Farmer, for the Over-lengths of Broadcloths; was pleased to descend so far, as to be a continual guest at Sanderson's House, then in London and Layton in Essex; and his best friend, it seems; whither he brought his Wife a Guest, himself then in disgrace concerning her,(I will be civill). And as Sir Walter's occasions had need (Courtiers being not over nice to make them often) he engaged Sanderson for him in £16000 and was indebted besides to Sanderson, in several summes of mony, as his Cash-books do yet evidence, amounting to £4000".[3]

Despite no direct evidence, it is not difficult to conjecture, how the private banker role expanded easily to become "man of business" and "treasurer". Both men saw opportunities; for Ralegh obtaining, free of charge, the services of a top calibre businessman, with "undoubted credit" in the City of London, to see that his extravagant life-style and a continuous stream of "projects" were funded in an orderly manner; for Sanderson being publicly linked, professionally as well as by marriage, with the best-known, if not the most popular, man in England. Many of Ralegh's plans would appeal to Sanderson as patriotic, even if, for Ralegh, this meant his personal power, glory and wealth at least as much as the advancement of England's and the Queen's interests.

The "honorary" nature of Sanderson's treasurership is perhaps echoed in the "Instructions to His Son and to Posterity" which Ralegh is thought to have written during his early years in the Tower (though they were not printed and published until 1632).when his son Wat was entering his teens. The cynical and materialistic tone of the Instructions has often been noted. One of the specific pieces of advice was that it is best to determine at the outset the duties and remuneration of "servants". Was Ralegh thinking of his employment of his nephew-in-law? Arrangements with "friends", or business arrangements which are not spelled out, do have a tendency to unravel under pressure or in changed circumstances, and this is what eventually happened to Ralegh and Sanderson; though the rupture was due, not to any failure to fix the duties or remuneration, but, as we will see, to Ralegh's deliberate actions, based either on a desire to injure Sanderson or on indifference as to what happened to him. When the two men fell out, in 1595, Ralegh had enjoyed 10 or 11 years of devoted and successful professional service from Sanderson, without having to pay for it.

In Appendix D the role of a treasurer or financial manager is explained and an attempt is made to construct an approximate cashflow for Ralegh's "operations" during the years from 1584–1595, combining his "domestic" and "public" expenditures in a corporate style presentation labelled "Ralegh Home & Colonial Enterprises". While obviously incomplete and "guesstimated" the cashflow provides a backdrop which enables us to provide credible answers to some vital questions, for example, Could Ralegh, on his own without Sanderson's help, have achieved what he did in the 1584–95 period? Did Ralegh fail to pay Sanderson what he owed him because he did not have the funds or because he chose not to do so?

Sanderson's marriage to Margaret Snedall seems to have been prosperous and happy at least for some twenty years, when financial difficulties arose. There is a pathetic description, in the defence filed by the moneylender to whom Sanderson had recourse, of Mrs Sanderson having to go, accompanied by her children, to the moneylender's house to ask for a further loan, because Sanderson was in a debtors' prison in respect of other debts: not a dignified experience for the wife of a City grandee. They stayed in the large house in Thames Street for about eight years and then moved around 1591 out of the City to the village of Newington Butts, about 1½ miles south of London Bridge.[4] They retained and used the family country house at Leyton in Essex[5] and, according to Sir William in An Answer, frequently entertained Ralegh and his wife Bess there.

Altogether, the Sandersons had seven sons and one daughter, Jane. She married well but seems to have died young, since her husband Sir John Woolley of the Privy Chamber is soon found remarried. Of the sons Ralegh, Cavendish, and Sir William stayed in England: the other four (Drake, Thomas, Hugh and Anthony) sought their fortunes overseas; perhaps following their father's patriotism – though it is difficult to see no connection with their father's financial crash in the 1605–1610 period and the resulting embarrassment and shortage of ready money.

Ralegh, the eldest son, as heir to his father, was pressed into joining with his father in mortgaging family property to meet his father's debts. He seems also to have had financial problems of his own,[6] and appears not to have married. Cavendish was a lawyer: he married and produced two sons and a daughter. An account of Sir William has already been given. Of the others,[7] Drake died at Dominica in the West Indies; Thomas married and had three children, and became a famous and successful mercenary soldier "eight years A Commander with the Dutch against the Portugalls in the East-Indies, and then in Ireland, Scotland, Sweden, Germany and lastly (but the first Colonell) that ever carried a double Regiment of 2000 men by sea, about the Norway Cape, to the Emperor of Mosco, in service at Smolensk, against the Poles, where he was basely murdered by that Scot Sir David

Lesly"[8] Sir William describes the fates of *three* additional brothers (but without identifying them), as follows "Another son cast away on the Coast of America, called then Norombega: Another, in discovery of the North-west passage, with Captain Weymouth, Another in the East-Indies". Death in the East Indies appears, from the terms of his will, to match with Hugh who died in 1624. This leaves Anthony and perhaps Raleigh.[9]

Part Two
Best Friend and Honorary Treasurer

We have now brought Sanderson and Ralegh together in 1584 or shortly thereafter: Sanderson in that year was 36, Ralegh 32 (Ralegh was, incidentally, knighted in 1584)…The third of our principal players, Thomas Harriot, aged 24 in 1584, had been part of Ralegh's household since around 1583; his first task being to teach navigation to Ralegh's sea captains in Durham House, the magnificent grace and favour mansion on the Thames, belonging to the Bishop of Durham, but made available by the Queen to Ralegh. In addition, he helped to manage Ralegh's ships and advised on their design and carried out accounting and financial duties. It seems that he was left some time to pursue his mathematical and scientific interests. He soon became deeply involved in the Roanoke project, working with John White to record American flora and fauna and identify possible commercial products, interpreting in negotiations with the native Americans (he mastered their language and produced a phonetical manual), and writing the famous Brief and True Report of the new found land of Virginia. Later, he worked wih John White on surveying Ralegh's allocated estates in Munster, both men being awarded tenancies by Ralegh.[1] After 1595 Harriot divided his loyalty between Ralegh and the 9th Earl of Northumberland – apparently to the satisfaction of both patrons.

Before moving forwards, a brief summing-up may be appropriate. At the time of their meeting Ralegh and Sanderson had both achieved success and were "rising men" in their respective spheres, the Court and the City, so that there was no competition between them; and a successful commercial/financial relationship, based on their complementary strengths, might be expected to develop, in addition to their kinship by marriage and close personal friendship.

While both were already successful, it is, however, appropriate to reflect on the nature of the contrasting arenas in which they had made their marks, and the personal characteristics which had brought this about. In Northern European trade and the City of London Sanderson had made his way by unremitting toil, meticulous attention to detail and close attention to personal relationships – the "steady" characteristics of any mercantile community. He appears, by the time of his marriage, never "to have put a foot wrong" – as a trainee factor, a merchant in his own right, becoming a "merchant adventurer" on his return to London, as a member (and assistant) of the Fishmongers' Company, and in his choice of a bride. A steady upward progress – which might be expected in due course to lead to preferment in the civic government of the City. Ralegh's choice of the profession of arms (in France and Ireland), with a spell at Oxford and then a plunge into the opportunistic jungle of the Court called for quite different qualities – for example, personal bravery, leadership, ruthlessness, continuous risk-taking, a lively wit and a heavy reliance on personal charm. Ralegh certainly displayed these, and indeed other admirable quailities, but he seems always to have overplayed his hand – to-day he might be called "over the top". In Ireland, his apparent enthusiasm for the Smethick massacre and his blatant insubordination towards the senior command were unlikely to win friends: instead of acting the peniless West Country gentleman rising by merit, he assumed the intolerable arrogance which was much commented on, seeming to relish making enemies quite unnecessarily; used his wit to enrage his elders and betters, and made no effort to conceal his financial ambitions and his tendency to abandon the truth when under pressure. While it may be apocryphal, Aubrey's account of his behaviour towards his fellow undergraduate at Oriel ("Mr Child of Worcestershire") – taking his gown and refusing either to return it or pay for it – neatly catches Ralegh's arrogance and selfishness at an early age.

Having now brought together out three main actors, and summarised their backgrounds and characters[2] we can now describe the three voyages of John Davies seeking the NW Passage. Sanderson was his main patron and financial backer although Ralegh was also an investor.

7

John Davis and the North West Passage

The report on NE Passage voyages over the previous 30 years which Sanderson commissioned and received in 1583[1] was not particularly encouraging and the Muscovy Company had by then switched from seeking a NE Passage to concentrating on developing trade with Russia. Frobisher had gone to the NW side a decade earlier, and this direction must have already seemed a better bet: The Gilberts and Ralegh (they were half brothers) had grown up in Devon with John Davis, the skilful seaman and navigator, who was to take charge. Accordingly some meetings on the feasibility of a NW Passage were held in January 1583 at Mortlake, at the house of Dr. John Dee, the savant skilled, among other things, in cartography and navigation, and a supporter of exploration and colonial settlement, between Walsingham, Adrian Gilbert and John Davis. Sanderson did not attend these meetings, but seems to have been recruited as lead financier soon afterwards: his absence from the Mortlake meetings is usually cited to establish that this was his first involvement with the NW Passage.[2] Once involved, Sanderson energetically and generously supported John Davis in all three voyages, providing one and possibly two ships of his own, definitely the Moonshine, and perhaps also the Sunshine,[3] and appointing as on-board representatives John Janes, who was his nephew, being the son of his sister Alice, and Henry Morgan. John Janes wrote accounts of the first and third voyages; and he was listed as "merchant" in the Sunshine in the first voyage. Henry Morgan wrote an account of the second voyage, being listed as "purser" in the Sunshine. John Janes seems to have taken to a seafaring life and clearly became devoted to John Davis; he served under him on his disastrous voyage accompanying Cavendish through the Magellan Strait in 1591–3 and was one of the handful of survivors. Janes wrote the account of that voyage, and, referring to John Davis, has Janes say "with whom and for whose sake I went this voyage"

Dr John Dee

Sanderson's support, not merely with money, was widely acknowledged.[5] Davis himself wrote "My worshipful good friend master William Sanderson, who of all men was the greatest adventurer in that action, and tooke such care for the performance thereof, that he hath to my knowledge at one time disbursed as much money as any five others whatsoever, out of his own purse, when some of the companie have bene slacke in giving their adventure".[6] While Sanderson was the main supporter there was a wide grouping of investors for the first voyage of John Davis, "Certaine Honourable personages and worthy Gentlemen of the Court and Countre, with divers worshipfull Marchants of London and the West Countrey…put downe their adventures" The other investors in the first voyage included Walsingham, Ralegh and the Merchant Adventurers of Exeter, who used their investment as a reason for declining to invest in Raleigh's Roanoke Expedition.[7]

Before describing the three voyages, we should mention a hidden agenda being pursued by the English Government with regard to the NW Passage exploration, additional to the desire to find a shorter route to the Pacific Ocean.[8] The plan, .probably derived originally from the treatise of Sir Humprey Gilbert in 1576, was to establish an English "forward base" beyond the Pacific end of the Passage, but well clear of the Spanish settlements on the West coast of North America in the region of California. It came to be called Nova Abion. This was to serve as (i) an English colony (ii) a commercial centre from which English merchants might trade, if the Spanish permitted (iii) alternatively, as a base from which the English might spoil the Spanish Empire in the Americas and the Philippines. We do not know how far these ideas had been developed when Frobisher made his voyages in the 1570s though on his second voyage he certainly had instructions and material to establish some kind of permanent English presence, and his crews were sworn to secrecy.[9] There is no indication that these ideas were pressed upon John Davis and his backers in the 1580s though since the principal political patron was the spymaster Sir Thomas Walsingham this seems likely. They certainly figured largely in the circumnavigations of Drake and Cavendish, and an elaborate plan of

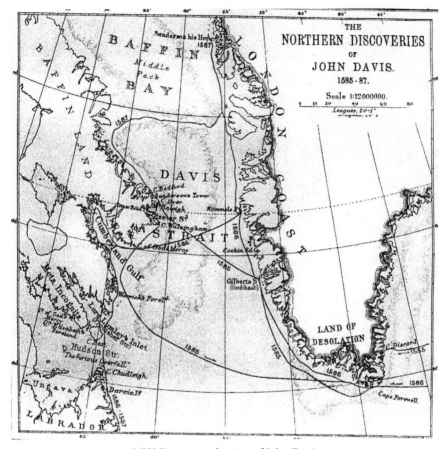

NW Passage exploration of John Davis

censorship and misinformation was hatched to conceal the seven months which Drake spent in 1579 exploring Northwards from California up to 57 degrees North. The plan involved withholding/re-writing accounts of the voyage and deliberately falsifying dates, distances, latitude and longitude figures and the charts themselves. Ironically, the Spanish, all along, had a good idea of what was afoot, from their intelligence in London and their meticulous collection of reports from Drake's progress up the West coasts of South and North America. It is clear that Drake discussed his instructions and plans quite freely with some of his prisoners. As a result, while the censorship, misinformation &c. was zealously managed in England, the truth was largely known in Europe, and the English authorities had to recognise this. On 16th October 1584 Sir Edward Stafford, the English ambassador in Paris, wrote to Sir Thomas Walsingham, "I find from Mr Hakluyt that Drake's journey is kept very secret in England, but here is in

Nova Albion, the English forward base selected by Drake in 1579

everyone's mouth". Richard Hakluyt was then serving as secretary to the ambassador but always kept himself fully informed about the activities of mariners and cartographers, both in England and Europe. If the true situation was public knowledge in Paris, it could not have failed to reach Madrid as well. In the event, no NW Passage was established, so the Nova Albion plan proved to be "a secret that never was".

The campaign of censorship and misinformation impacted on the Molyneux terrestrial globes which Sanderson was to finance a few years later.[10]

The first expedition of John Davis consisted of two small ships, the Sunshine and Moonshine (certainly one and possibly both belonging to Sanderson) and 42 men, and left Dartmouth on 7th June 1585. They were held up for 12 days in the Scilly Isles by contrary winds, so Davis, characteristically, with the master and John Janes, surveyed and charted all the islands. Davis had never sailed in Northern waters before but he made a landfall on the south east coast of Greenland on 20th July, naming it from its daunting appearance "Desolation". He then proceeded round the southern tip of Greenland and up the west coast, and entered and named Gilbert Sound at around 64' N, making friendly contact with some native Inuit. Sailing on NW at the end of July they anchored on 6th July at 66' 40" N "in a very fair rode ... voyde from ye pester of yce". The anchorage was named Totnes Road, and the sheltering bluff Mount Raleigh. Going ashore they killed three polar bears. By this time they had crossed the Davis Strait and were on the American side on the Baffin Island coast. Turning back to the South, they sailed some 60 leagues[11] NW into Cumberland Sound, and then some 20 leagues SW into an inlet. At this time, around 18th August "considering that the yeere was spent for this was in the fine of August…we took it our best course to returne with notice of our good successe for this small time of Search"[12], and accordingly set course for home. By 10thSeptember they were again off South Greenland, and on 27thSeptember sighted England, entering Dartmouth on the 30th Davis made an optimistic report to Walsingham, "The north-west passage is a matter nothing doubtful…the sea navigable, void of yse, the ayre tolerable, and the waters very depe". He also reported "an yle of very grate quantytie, not in any globe or map dyscrybed, yielding a sufficient trade of furre and lether".[13]

The second voyage set out from Dartmouth on 7th May 1586, the cost of £1175 having been raised mainly in the West Country[14] The fleet consisted of the Mermaid (120 tonnes), the Sunshine, a barke of 60 tonnes, the Moonshine (misdescribed as Moonlight), a barke of 35 tonnes) and a 10 tonne pinnace Northstarre. The account of the voyage was written by Davis himself.

When the fleet reached 60' N Davis detached the Moonshine and the Northstarre – the Mermaid deserted the fleet at this point – to sail northward between Greenland and Iceland. They visited Iceland and reported very plentiful fishing. They then sailed to Greenland and reached Gilbert's Sound, which was the agreed rendezvous. Relations with the Inuit were mixed. With no sign of the rest of the fleet, they set out for England. The Moonshine reached the Thames on 6thOctober, but the Northstarre pinnace was lost on the way home. The account of this side trip was written by Sanderson's servant Henry Morgan, who was serving as purser in the Moonshine.

On 15th June Davis made a landfall on Greenland at around 60' N 47'W. To clear the land and ice lying off they sailed SW and worked back north to Gilbert Sound, visited in the previous year: the Inuit were again friendly, recognising some of the English faces. Some exploration on land and up rivers was undertaken. The friendly atmosphere was soured by Inuit stealing. Sailing north they encountered a massive iceberg and a barrier of ice on 17th July, around 63' 40"N. Coasting along the barrier the ships became iced up and the crews became sick so by the end of July they bore ESE and by 1st.August found land free of ice, warm and pestered with mosquitoes around 66'33"N. This was evidently on the Greenland side. On 12th August they set course due west and sailed some 70 leagues to an island where they anchored and then on the 15th set course south and on the 18th found "land North west from us….being a vert fayre promontory" in 65' N – probably Cape Walsingham. From here they sailed south looking for "openings" to the west. When they reached 57', 56' and 55' N there were great stocks of cod fish: thirty couple were caught and salted to take back to

England. Some of these fish, on Walsingham's instructions, were presented to Lord Burghley, thus moving him to encourage Davis' exploration. On 6th September a shore party went to pick up fish which they had stored on an island: they were ambushed and at least two men killed. Strong winds from the north built up and on the 11th September they set course for England, arriving at Dartmouth on 4th October. Within 10 days Davis wrote to Sanderson to report that 500 seal skins and 140 half skins had been obtained by trade. He was now confident that the NW passage was "in one of foure places, or els not at all".

For the third voyage, which departed from Dartmouth on 19th May 1587, all the Western merchants and most of those in London "fell from the Action".[15] There were three ships, the Elizabeth of Dartmouth, the Sunshine of London (which we have already met, a bark of 60 tonnes, probably belonging to Sanderson) and the Eillin of London: she was clinker built i.e. with overlapping planks, and seems to have been much smaller than the other two, being described as a pinnace. The plan was to leave two ships "at the place of fishing" (identified in the second voyage), in order to make some money to underwrite the cost of the expedition, with instructions to meet up with Davis at the end of August, while he sailed north to continue the exploration. Surprisingly, it looks as though Davis chose the Ellin for himself: despite her poor performance: she was unflatteringly described by Janes "At sea she was like to a cart drawn with oxen" since in light airs she had to be towed.[16] The account of the voyage was written by John Janes, described as "servant to...Master William Sanderson" The fleet made a landfall in Greenland on 14th June and by 16th June seem to have been back at Gilbert Sound, where they were welcomed by the Inuit: another fine piece of navigation from England. On 21st. June Davis in Ellin set off north up the west coast of Greenland. At 67' N they could see both Greenland and America, and feared that they were in a gulf, but at 68' the passage widened. By 30[th]June they had reached 72' 11" N. "the sea all open to the Westwards and Northwards". The wind turning northerly they named that piece of land Hope Sanderson, set course W and sailed for more than 40 leagues when on 2nd. July they met a "mighty banke of Ice" running north-south. For several days they tried to sail round or through the ice barrier without success, and they turned back towards the south. Davis' own comment must be noted[17] "I was constrained to coast the same toward the South, not seeing any shore West from me, neither was there any yce towards the North, but a great sea, free, large, very salt and blew, and of an unsearchable depth". . On 19th July they sighted Mount Raleigh (on Baffin Island) and by midnight that night were off "the streights which we discovered the first yeere" i.e. Cumberland Gulf. On 23rd. July they sailed 60 leagues NW into the strait and the following day turned about sailing SE "to recover the Sea". At noon on 29th July they were "cleare out of the streights" in 64' N. On 30th July they "passed by a great banke or inlet, which lay between 63' and 62' N, which we called Lumleis Inlet (almost certainly Frobisher Strait). On 31[st.] July they passed a headland named Warwikes Foreland, and "This day and night we passed by a very great gulfe, the water whirling and roring, as it were the meeting of tides". Davis' own account is even more dramatic, "In which place we had 8 or 9 great rases, currents or overfals, lothsomly crying like the rage of the waters under London bridge, and bending their course into the sayde gulf"[18] This disturbed water seems to have been the "Furious Overfalls" as they were described on the New World Map of Edward Wright and the Molyneux terrestrial globes – marking the entrance to Hudson Strait. On the 1st August they named the southern cape, at the mouth of Hudson Strait, at 61' N. Chudleis Cape (after Davis' Devon colleague John Chudley) By 15th August they were almost to 51" N., the designated rendezvous with the fishing vessels, but the latter were not there nor had they left any marks as had been agreed. After 16 days fishing they had sailed back to England. Davis therefore set course for England and arrived at Dartmouth on 15th September 1587. True to form, the very next day Davis wrote to Sanderson in upbeat mood. "I....have sailed threescore leagues further than my determination at my departure. I have been in 73 degrees, finding the Sea all open, and forty leagues between land and land. The passage is most probable, the execution easie, as at my coming you shall fully know". He commented, later, "By this last discovery it seemed most manifest that the passage was free and without impediment toward the North: but by reason of the Spanish fleet (i.e. the Armada) and unfortunate time of (Walsingham's) death, the voyage was omitted and never sithins attempted...How far I proceeded and in what forme this discovery lieth, doth appear upon the Globe which Master Sanderson to his very great charge hath published, for the which he deserveth great favour and commendation."[19] The Molyneux globes were published in 1592 but work had started some years earlier, and Hakluyt hailed their expected publication in the first edition of his Principle Navigations in 1589

Reading these abridged accounts of the three voyages (and even the full versions) may give the impression that not a lot happened and not much was achieved. Davis' calibre can however be set in context by reading the accounts of other pre-1600 Arctic voyages, where much more "went wrong" and it is often impossible to know where the expeditions actually were at any given moment. Davis suffered some serious blows – the pinnace Northstarre was lost on the voyage home in 1586, the Mermaid deserted in the same year, the fishermen disobeyed orders and sailed home in 1587; but, on the other hand, there were very few casualties, virtually no damage to the ships, Davis went largely where he intended, pack ice excepted, maintained on the whole, despite provocations, good relations with the Inuit, kept excellent navigational and geographical records and was by all accounts a much respected commander who had no trouble in maintaining discipline and, by contemporary standards, "a happy ship".

The threat posed by the Armada and the death of Sir Francis Walsingham put an end to English searches for the NW Passage for some years, but there is no doubt that Davis' navigational knowledge, when combined with his seamanship and command skills, provided the outstanding contribution to that exploration prior to 1600. Davis published a popular manual on navigation, The Seaman's Secrets, first issued in 1594 and frequently re-published, and a reasoned case for the NW Passage entitled, The Worlde's Hydrographical Description in 1595; but by that date English interest had waned. He invented a "Backstaff" (sometimes called "Davis's Quadrant"), an improved instrument for measuring the altitude of heavenly bodies, which remained in use until Hadley's reflecting quadrant in the 18th century, followed by the sextant.[20] The "Traverse Book" which Davis kept on his third voyage has set the model for ships' logs ever since, and the maps and notes on navigation, the Inuit and flora and fauna which he brought back from his Arctic voyages testify to his professionalism. The other explorers displayed great courage and seamanship but were often unable to explain where they had been. While acting as fleet pilot to the first fleet of the East India Company (1601–3) Davis seems to have passed on his enthusiasm for the NW Passage to Sir James Lancaster, since he, with a group of prominent City men led by Sir Thomas Smythe, incorporated as "The Company of Merchants of London, Discoverers of the North-West Passage", sent out Henry Hudson (on his last voyage) in 1610, Button in 1612, Hall in the same year and Bylot and Baffin in 1615 and 1616.

John Davis, Emmery Molyneux and John Norden were all outstanding in their respective fields – we may conclude that Sanderson picked winners, not by chance or luck, but by selecting them carefully. We know more about his relationship with Davis than with the other two, and it seems that Sanderson was the best type of investment banker who looks not just for potential profit (in the event, none of the three situations seem to have turned a profit) but for ability, professionalism and personal chemistry as well. While Davis always displays proper respect for his patron, theirs was obviously a warm relationship. A particularly attractive aspect is that Davis shared navigational discussions with Sanderson, who was certainly interested in this subject.[21] While not a professional, Sanderson seems also to have been quite knowledgeable – he must have had plenty of experience in shipping from his days as an expatriate merchant in North Europe, and to have added to this as owner of his small merchant ships. Later, he was involved in managing the Roanoke voyages and the preparation of Raleigh's 1595 expedition to Manao/El Dorado.

Before leaving the NW Passage it is appropriate to mention, as an ironic footnote, that (with one or two exceptions, for example, the independently minded Sir William Monson) no one analysed with vigour the distinction between the two questions (i) Does a Northern passage exist? and (ii) If it does, Is it commercially viable? The very short Arctic summer and the unpredictability of the ice would have made a one-way passage impossible to plan with any certainty, and a two-way passage a dangerous gamble. This may have been due to the fact that the "decision-takers" were merchants, not seamen; with the exception of Sir James Lancaster, who, while a very experienced naval commander, had never sailed in Arctic waters. Conversely, John Davis, despite his experience of Arctic conditions (albeit undertaken in the summer months) convinced himself that ice was not really a problem,[22] but until he went to the East with Houtman and Lancaster, following the conventional route round the Cape, he had no experience of the sheer length of these longer trading trips and the impossibility of planning months in advance. It may have been doubts over the commercial viability of the NW Passage, assuming that it existed, that led Lancaster, towards the end of his life (he died in 1618), to urge the East India Company to develop an alternative route to the East Indies westabout via the Magellan Strait.

From the Northern Pasages we move to the North Atlantic to describe the Roanoke settlement in Virginia. Here Ralegh was the prime mover, with Sanderson playing a supporting role as his banker and treasurer. Given Ralegh's vision and energy, it is sad that the Queen felt unable to permit him to lead the expedition in person: had she done so the outcome might have been quite different. From an English point of view the expedition, while exciting, was a failure, but in America it has always attracted extraordinary interest as the first substantial English settlement on the continent.

8

The Roanoke Settlement

Sir Humphrey Gilbert addressed a Discourse to the Queen in 1576, favouring a NW rather than a NE Passage as a short cut to the Pacific Ocean, and was granted a patent to discover and explore the north parts of America. Following his death in 1583 a new patent was granted to his brother Adrian, and the three voyages led by John Davis in 1585, 1586 and 1587[1] were planned under this patent, with the political support of Sir Francis Walsingham, the Secretary of State, and the financial backing of Sanderson and others. Ralegh had thought of becoming involved with Humphrey Gilbert but when he was lost at sea in 1583, Ralegh persuaded the Queen to split the territory of the patent, at 50 degrees North: while the more northerly coast was licensed to Adrian Gilbert, Ralegh himself in 1584 received the re-issued patent to acquire and occupy land in North America further South. His overall aim throughout his life (perhaps originally inspired by Drake) was to promote the Imperial Vision already described, though for Ralegh glory for Queen Elizabeth and England was closely tied to the acquisition of wealth and power for himself. The argument ran, Taking booty from the Spanish and Portuguese is fine but it would be better to replace English piracy (sometimes legitimised as privateering) by settlement. Further, this course would enable England to compete directly with Spain and Portugal, acquiring the riches of America at their source and on an ongoing basis; and providing settlement opportunities for English people whether adventurous, disaffected or criminal. The Imperial Vision would be realised through superior sea power. "The constant burden of [Ralegh's] song is 'Let us get for Her Majesty a better, richer Indies of our own".[2]

Others shared Raleigh's vision, particularly those in his immediate circle[3] and it is interesting to observe how over many years Raleigh orchestrated an advertising and public relations campaign to promote his aims. In prose, his own works were supplemented by that of Sir Humphrey Gilbert ("Discourse" presented to the Queen in 1576), Hakluyt ("Divers Voyages touching the Discoveries of America" 1582; "A Particular Discourse Concerning Western Planting", presented to the Queen in 1584; "A Notable History concerning four voyages made by Certain French Captains into Florida" 1587; Prefaces to editions of Peter Martyr and Laudonniere 1587; Preface to the "Principle Discoveries" 1598); Sir George Peckham ("A True Report of the Late Discoveries...of the Newfound Landes ...by Sir Hunphrey Gilbert" 1583); Arthur Barlow, Report from Roanoke 1584; Ralph Lane (the first governor), a letter to Richard Hakluyt "from the new fort in Virginia" 1586; Thomas Harriot ("A Brief and True Report of the new found land of Virginia" 1588 (translated subsequently into Latin, French and German), Lawrence Keymis ("A Relation of the Second Voyage to Guiana" 1596), while in verse he enlisted Spencer, Chapman, Roydon, Drayton, Marlowe and perhaps Arthur Gorges. Two examples of promotional poetry must suffice.[4]

From Drayton's "To the Virginian Voyage"
("The whole poem is all but a verse paraphrase of Harriot's True Report")[5]

> And cheerfully at Sea
> Successe you still intice
>   To get the Pearle and Gold
>   And ours to hold
> Virginia,
> Earth's onely Paradise

From Chapman's Carmen Epicum De Guiana 1596

> Riches, and conquest, and renoun I sing,
> Riches with honour, conquest without blood,
> Enough to seat the Monarchy of earth,
> Like to Jove's eagle, on Eliza's hand.
> Guiana, whose rich feet are mines of gold,
> Whose forehead knocks against the roof of stars,
> Stands tiptoes at fair England looking,
> Kissing her hand, bowing her mighty breast,
> And every sign of all submission making,
> To be her sister and the daughter both
> Of our most sacred Maid.

The advertising campaign was "spiced up" by Ralegh personally promoting the use of potatoes and tobacco, and by bringing native Americans to England. The continual references to "Gold", particularly in the writings on South America, may also be noted.[6] In rounding off the description of "Ralegh as publicist" the American author of Raleigh and Marlowe concludes (on p.306) "He was practical enough to believe even then that it paid to advertise".

With his renewed North American patent in 1584 it appears that Ralegh was pursuing two immediate objectives in parallel (i) a self-sufficient English settlement and (ii) a naval/military base from which the Spanish colonies and their treasure fleets might be attacked. This meant going as far south as possible to avoid the extreme climate of the American north east but not too close to existing Spanish settlements in Florida.

The site chosen at Roanoke was flawed from the outset, since on an exposed coast there was no safe deep water harbour or anchorage. Further, until the third settlement in 1587, there were no tradesmen or agriculturalists included to establish and maintain a settlement: the organisation was on military lines – nothing in itself wrong with that – but the "settlers" were to rely on the native Americans to provide shelter, food and so on – a recipe for disaster, as events proved. Once the settlement got

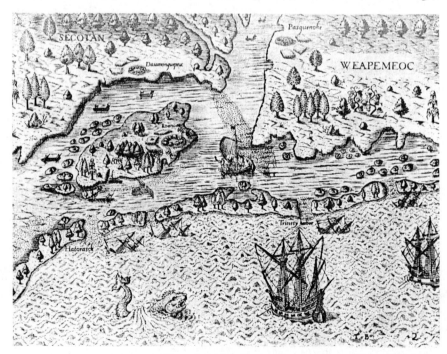

Roanoke. Note the wrecks

into trouble efforts to relieve it were feeble and ineffective, though, to be fair to Ralegh, relief efforts were thwarted by national measures in the face of the Armada. Had he been permitted by the Queen to leave England to take charge of his colony either at the outset or when things started to go wrong, his dynamic energy and bravery might have recovered the situation.[7]

The description of the new territory by Thomas Harriot ("A Full and True Description") has always been admired, but the emphasis on the attractions awaiting the settlers and the omission/denigration of the less enthusiastic views of men who had actually been there downgraded a brilliant multi-disciplinary account to a misleading prospectus. At the same time, it is suggested that Harriot should not be criticised for what he was doing – loyally pursuing his master's obvious objectives; if any criticism is to be levelled or blame allocated for "spinning" or misrepresentation, it must, in this case as in others, be attached to the "directing mind". Similar considerations apply to the "Discovery of Guyana", published in 1596, where Harriot was engaged to support his master's "line" that the 1595 expedition was (i) a special brand of enlightened exploration, designed to protect the native population from Spanish exploitation and deliver them to the benign rule of Queen Elizabeth (ii) that, therefore, Guyana must be "reserved" as a Ralegh "sphere of influence", protected from development by other Englishmen who (unlike Ralegh) would be rapacious, and (iii) that even the maps and charts must be officially "kept under wraps" to discourage exploitation by others.[8]

The first settlement was installed on Roanoke Island in July 1585 by Ralegh's cousin Sir Richard Grenville, who left Ralph Lane, an army officer, in command. Some financial subscriptions were raised to meet the cost, in which Sanderson no doubt figured. Carew Ralegh, Ralegh's brother, tried unsuccessfully, to obtain financial support from the Merchant Adventurers of Exeter in January 1585: they pleaded that they were already invested in John Davis' second voyage to the NW Passage, of which the main supporter was Sanderson.[9] In addition, privateering was planned as a source of cash, and the voyage was routed via the West Indies for this purpose, as well as to pick up fresh food and water, livestock and plants. By July 1586 the Roanoke settlers were short of food and took passage home with Sir Francis Drake, when he visited the colony. The advance relief vessel despatched by Ralegh missed them by a few days, and the main relief fleet under Grenville arrived about a month later: he left behind 15 men who were never seen again. Grenville's squadron took some prizes which probably covered his costs. The returning colonists voiced different opinions – the leaders Lane, Harriot and White were positive, the majority critical and disgruntled. Ralegh therefore changed tack and planned a new settlement, based on farming, volunteers and land allocations, in the Chesapeake Bay area, to be led by White. Early in 1587 Ralegh by charter established a company to carry this into effect, but retained overall control himself. The expedition made a landfall in America in July 1587 and, after some command problems, arrived at Roanoke in August to find the old settlement destroyed. The naval commander, the Portuguese Fernandez, refused to take the party and their stores beyond Roanoke, so the important objective of finding a deep water haven or mooring was abandoned. After further disagreements White set sail back to England on 22nd August to organise reinforcements. Ralegh at once started to organise a relief expedition, again under Grenville, but this was delayed until early 1588 when in April only two pinnaces were permitted to sail because of the impending Armada attack. They attempted some privateering on the voyage out, were badly mauled and had to return, only a month later, in May. On 5th October 1587 Ralegh and Sanderson had jointly borrowed £1,500 from Sir Thomas Smythe.[10] Because the loan was negotiated at a time when the ongoing Virginia operation was needing cash, this was probably the main reason for it, but nothing more could be done in 1588. In March 1589 Ralegh organised additional investors into the settlement Company, including Sanderson himself, Sir Thomas Smythe, senior, and other London merchants, and Richard Hakluyt,[11] but no actual expedition was actually put together until the end of the year, only to have the plan thwarted by a national embargo in February 1590. The cause of the delay throughout 1589 is not known, though it may have been due to the surge of activity in privateering, which promised better prospects for profit. The deadlock was broken early in 1590 by Ralegh obtaining offical permission to set sail, while Sanderson, who contributed one, or possibly two, small ships of his own, negotiated a loan of £5,000 from John Watts, a major merchant backer of privateering, with an understanding that the relief expedition would join forces with Watts' three ships destined for privateering. Setting out in March 1590 this expedition sailed via the West Indies, where prizes were taken, and arrived at Roanoke by mid–August, to find no trace of the colonists, except a sign suggesting that they had moved to nearby Croataon. That marked the end of the Roanoke settlements, but one of the prizes taken by Watts on the 1590 voyage (the Buen Jesus) involved litigation in the Admiralty Court in 1591, in which Watts succeeded in depriving Sanderson's ship (the Moonlight alias Mery Terlayne) of any share in the booty. Since Sanderson and Watts were on friendly terms – and Watts also wanted to exclude a third claimant – it has been suggested that they may have concluded a side-deal.[12]

It is usually assumed that Sanderson commenced acting as "Honorary Treasurer" to Ralegh in 1586 or 1587 since Sanderson in 1587 negotiated the loan from Customer Smythe mentioned above. However, if it is accepted that Sanderson started to support Ralegh financially when he got to know him at or soon after his (Sanderson's) marriage in 1584, the correct start date might be a year or two earlier, perhaps in 1585. From a financial poit of view there was really no distinction between Ralegh's "domestic" and "public" projects. We saw above that Ralegh sent his brother Carew to solicit financial support for the Roanoke settlement from the Exeter Merchants in 1585, only to be rejected because, they explained, they had recently invested in the second voyage of Adrian Gilbert and John Davis, and wished to see the outcome of that voyage before considering further investment. It might be argued that, since Carew was sent, rather than Sanderson, the latter had not at that date commenced to act for Ralegh. On the other hand, Ralegh may have reckoned that a member of the Ralegh family would get a better hearing from West Country merchants than a Londoner like Sanderson. If he thought that, he was almost certainly mistaken, since there was considerable feeling in Exeter against Ralegh because of his monopoly exactions.[13] Alternatively, the Exeter men may have decided that they simply did not want to support Ralegh, and used their existing investment as a diplomatic excuse. The exact commencement of Sanderson's activities as unpaid treasurer is not too important, since it seems that, until the quarrel in 1595, Sanderson somehow always managed to "find the money", either out of incoming cash flow or from loans or by putting up his own cash . Certainly, as Sanderson pointed out in the litigation in 1611–13, there had been no complaints about his performance during the period of his treasurership.[14]

We now pass back across the North Atlantic to Ireland to describe the Munster Plantation. – designed by the government to tap the current enthusiasm in England for investing risk capital overseas. To-day it may look strange to regard Virginia and Munster as potential competing investments but at the time this was certainly the case, with similar government objectives, the same technical terms, the same methods for raising money, even the same touts employed to drum up the settlers.[15] Ralegh was to be by far the largest investor in Munster.

9

The Munster Plantation[1]

At the end of the Desmond rebellion in 1586 it appeared that some 600,000 acres belonging to Desmond and his supporters were available for confiscation by the Crown. Accordingly, senior ministers in London devised this bold scheme of "plantation" to pacify the area at minimum cost to the Crown: it was based on tapping the current enthusiasm in England for investing risk capital in overseas trade and colonial settlement.

Munster was not the first, nor the last, scheme to colonise or settle Ireland, and there were many theories and ideas as to how this might best be done.[2]

The scheme was planned in some detail, but, in the event, various modifications were made or simply tolerated. The overall objective was to make a fresh start in the area affected, introducing English local government and English law, particularly as affecting real property, English language and English dress. After excluding "mountains, bogs and barren heath" the land was divided into 12,000 acre units ("seignories") which were offered on favourable terms – low land prices, initially reduced rents, freedom from customs duties and so on. The government issued invitations to prominent men in all the counties of England (and in Wales), initially targeting landowners, particularly younger sons and younger brothers, but later adding senior officials and army officers, many with direct experience of Ireland – to become "undertakers" and acquire a seignory, effectively as a "tenant in chief" of the Crown. The undertakers were each obliged to settle 91 families, including six freeholders, copyholders, farmers and cottagers in every seignory, with a complete spread of farming and other skills and all necessary tools, household equipment, weapons, provisions and so on. In the event the investment cost of establishing a seignory seems to have worked .out at around £1,000.[3] A maximum of one seignory per undertaker was set, but Ralegh eventually, by February 1586, had been allotted 3½ seignories, some 42,000 acres, by the Queen's decision. His original allocation in 1585 was the area on the lower right bank of the Blackwater River including Youghal, probably the most fertile, and attractive, area of the whole plantation; and he improved his new Irish estates by making additional purchases.

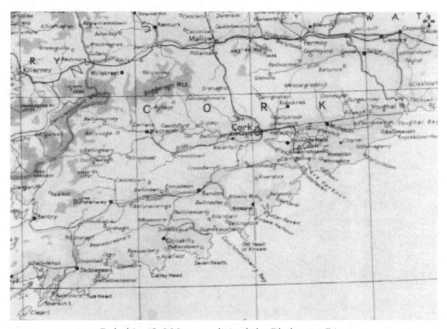

Ralegh's 42,000 acres adjoined the Blackwater River

Without the need for hindsight, it seems reasonably clear that the scheme, as planned, could last only until the native Irish recovered their strength – since it was based on ethnic cleansing and apartheid: the Irish were to be cleared from the area by the sword or expulsion and none was to be included in the new settlement. This was recognised by providing that the new settlers should be armed and should fortify their buildings, and that English troops would provide protection. In the event the military protection was quickly scaled down and the settler militia reached only 20% of its paper strength, so that in 1598 most of the settlers fled into the towns or back to England or were expelled by the Irish.

Once the seignories had been awarded, at least four further major problems arose. First, the area of the land available proved to be substantially less than had been expected. Confiscation was challenged in a large number of cases, with complex arguments based on both Irish customary law and English land law, so that only some 300,000 acres remained, which were apportioned among 35 undertakers. Secondly, there proved to be insufficient English (and Welsh) tradesmen and agricultural workers coming forward for the undertakers to fulfil their obligations. Thirdly, it turned out that a number of Irish were, in fact, still living in the area of the plantation: undertakers were happy to take them on as tenants since they did not require to be transported and equipped, they knew the land and their security of tenure was improved – so the original stipulation excluding Irish tenants was quietly dropped. Fourthly, the disputes over title and the shortage of surveyors delayed the government survey of the Plantation area, so that the undertakers and their tenants were occupying their acreage before their exact boundaries had been established and their patents issued. This uncertainty over exact boundaries gave rise to yet further legal disputes over title.

As a result of these problems a number of undertakers withdrew, but those who persisted were taking possession in 1587 and all were in occupation by 1588. Ralegh displayed his customary vision and energy. As already noted, he obtained 3½ times the maximum permitted acreage, the patents for his seignories were less strict in their terms than the others and his rents were lower. By 1589 he reported that he was well on the way to achieving his target number of tenants, (144 families out of 318) most from south west England but several being Irish. He installed Thomas Harriot in Molana Abbey (he sold out ten years later), and John White, the administrator (and illustrator) of the Roanoke settlement, was also awarded a tenancy nearby at Ballynoe in Kilmore. Ralegh employed Harriot and White to survey his seignories . The contention that Ralegh at this time introduced tobacco and the potato to Ireland is probably not true but he seems to have introduced cherry trees from the Azores; he attempted to introduce hops; in 1594 he brought over Cornish miners to extract iron ore and work an iron works at Youghal; established a salmon fishery, and started a flourishing factory which exported barrel staves for winemakers. By 1590 340,000 barrel staves had been exported but the factory was halted for two years by his enemy Lord Deputy Fitzwillliam; this was only one of his efforts to damage Ralegh. Improving Myrtle Grove in Youghal as a residence, Ralegh also started to re-built Lismore Castle in Youghal, apparently as a long-term "seat" to match his importance, and encouraged the anglicisation of his estates by changing the place-names. He re-named two manors Inchiquin Ralegh and Mogeley Ralegh[4] and encouraged his tenants to follow suit. His leases to his tenants all included an obligation to hedge, ditch and enclose – something the government was promoting. And in 1588–9 Ralegh was elected mayor of Youghal.

Leaving aside his energetic and enlightened initiatives as a landowner, it

Myrtle Grove, Ralegh's house at Youghal

is interesting to consider Ralegh's overall "investment plan" with regard to Munster. First, we may recall his consistent identification of his own acquisition of power and wealth with the advancement of the interests of the Queen and England – in the case of Munster the Queen seems to have acquiesced in this view! As an ambitious national figure, his only land-holding up to this time was the small family estate of Colaton Ralegh in Devon, and he was clearly sensitive about this, since he tried on several occasions to acquire a "seat", eventually succeeding with Sherborne, only to lose it on his attainder. When in Ireland as a soldier in 1581/2 he had tried, unsuccessfully, to buy Barryscourt Castle overlooking Cork Harbour. In 1584 he tried, again unsuccessfully, to buy his birthplace in Devon, Hayes Barton. It seems likely, therefore, that, with 42,000 acre estate acquired in Munster on privileged terms he wished to establish a mansion to match his importance, hence his plan, never completed, to re-build Lismore Castle.[5] Whether or not this deduction is correct it seems that by about 1589 Ralegh's interest in Ireland was on the wane. We do not know exactly why, but thre possible reasons may be suggested (i) he had succumbed to the alternative charms of Sherborne. He did not receive his 99 year lease of Sherborne until early in1592 but his interest had been aroused several years earlier and it took some time before the Queen identified a new compliant Bishop of Salisbury (ii) he became disappointed with the progress in developing his Irish properties: the embargo on the export of barrel staves, which was highly profitable, and other irritations stemming from a hostile Lord Deputy, might well have been factors. (iii) he became disappointed with the financial returns and/or needed funds for other purposes.

Apart from its larger size Ralegh's land-holding had another peculiar feature – no less than 18 of his tenants were London merchants. It seems impossible not to see here the hand of Sanderson, acting as Ralegh's man of business. It looks as though Ralegh, on his treasurer's advice, had deliberately sought out an additional source of capital, financial instead of agricultural investors, in order (i) to make up his complement as an undertaker and (ii) in this way to "lay off" some of the investment which he had already made. On this basis, he then sent out Sanderson among his City of London colleagues to find them.[6] It is possible that part of the "sales message" to the merchants was that "making a market" in Munster tenancies would be quite acceptable, so that an investment could be "sold on", and that, provided the tenanted land was stocked and worked it was not essential for the investor to settle in Ireland. Some support for this suggestion is provided by Sanderson's own actions. In 1592 he personally acquired the small seignory of Castletown (3274 acres) by purchase from the original undertaker, and then sold it on ten years later in 1602: it seems likely that he never visited his estate.[7]

At the later stage, when Ralegh's enthusiasm for Ireland was cooling (we have suggested that this started about 1589), a similar corporate finance "device" was deployed. Ralegh sold leases of parts of the estate to ten new investors in 1589 and a lease of the seignory itself in 1594 to another new investor. By taking a capital sum (a "fine") at the outset, followed by an appropriately reduced running rent, he started to recover part of his investment. Finally, in 1602, he sold out his seignory altogether to Robert Boyle for the low price of £1,500. Boyle then, to complete title to the seignory and recover possession of the leased areas, had to buy out the leases which Ralegh had granted. This apparently cost him an additional £2,500 though Boyle stated that he had to pay £2,700. Even at a cost of £4,200 Boyle got a bargain. While Ralegh's commitment had evidently disappeared, Boyle, being "on the spot" was confident of being able to improve the profitability of the estates after the Irish invasion of the settlement, which, with his energy and adoption of Ralegh's enlightened policies, he proceeded to do. He went on to acquire most of the remainder of the Munster Plantation land[8] and also developed industry throughout the area. When booming Irish land prices in the early 17th century were added to Boyle's efficient management and aggressive purchasing he became the richest man in the entire United Kingdom. Later still, in 1628, Bess Ralegh attempted to annul the sale to Boyle on the basis that Ralegh had been compelled to sell at an undervalue, but with some judicious bribes Boyle was able to fight off this challenge (as well as the attempt by the Crown to cancel the sale because of Ralegh's attainder).[9] Did Ralegh's investment in Ireland turn a profit? We do not know for certain. Obviously, with 3½ seignories he would not have had to find 3½ times the estimated average cost per seignory of £1,000.[10] We have already noted that his rent obligation was lower than the norm, and, for the original establishment in Munster, he could have used his own or Sanderson's ships at nominal cost. He did however make additional purchases. The export of barrel staves proved highly profitable, until halted. We may therefore conclude that the estate at least recovered what had been laid out. Sadly, however, the benefit of the energy and ingenuity displayed at the outset by Ralegh and Sanderson accrued to others – Boyle's second and third instalments of the original purchase price (together £1000) went to the Crown, under Ralegh's attainder, and the highly profitable 42,000 acres enriched Boyle and his descendants.[11]

Chapter 10
Molyneux's Globes

We turn now to describe Sanderson's major investment banking project – encouraging and financing Emmery Molyneux's globes. Ralegh was not an investor but he was clearly a strong supporter.

First, the project was part of the Imperial Vision already described. Ralegh, together with Humphrey Gilbert, Drake and Richard Hakluyt, had made the case for deploying scientists, mathematicians and other learned men to improve English navigational practices and instruments, following the example of the Portuguese and Spanish, as a means of enhancing English sea power as the instrument of overseas settlement. Hakluyt praised

Middle Temple Terrestrial Globe   *Middle Temple Celestial Globe*

Ralegh in glowing terms for his contribution, including the employment of Harriot, when he dedicated to Ralegh his edition of Peter Martyr's book in 1587.[1] Ralegh and Harriot formed part of the "networks" which Richard Hakluyt assembled and orchestrated to contribute both to the production of the globes and to the publication of his Principal Navigations – one network consisting of naval commanders and the other of mathematicians, astronomers, cartographers and so on. A third network assembled artisans, engravers and similar skilled tradesmen.

Secondly. the official manual for the use of Molyneux's globes, the "Tractatus de Globis", was written by Robert Hues and dedicated to Ralegh. Hues was well known to Ralegh, and became one of his executors, and through him met the 9th Earl of Northumberland who made him, like Harriot, a "gentleman pensioner".

As we have seen, in the 1580s Sanderson was busy both with John Davis' voyages and with the affairs of his uncle-in-law Ralegh. By around 1587 he had already identified another suitable target for his investment banking enthusiasm and his patriotism. It was the most attractive proposition so far – it had the potential to make money, it was highly patriotic, it would appeal to the Queen personally and it would promote and assist English overseas trade, exploration and settlement. The financing of the new globes, terrestrial and celestial, published by Emmery Molyneux, proved to be "an event of national importance".[2] In consequence Sanderson, as the patron and financial backer, became a national figure.

How did Molyneux, who had never, as far as we know, had any previous connection with cartography[3], come to conceive the idea? Although Drake and Cavendish had completed circumnavigations, in general England lagged well behind Europe in long-haul sea voyages and the leaders in cartography at this time were mainly to be found in the Low Countries.[4] Further, in their design and construction, globes are far more challenging than two dimensional maps or charts: they involve complicated mathematics as well as precision engineering skills in constructing a true sphere, mounting the globe on its stand and so on. A clue may be found in the fact that the Molyneux globes were very much a team effort, not the brainchild of a single outstanding cartographer. While we have no direct evidence, it may be suggested that the idea of publishing the English globes originated with Richard Hakluyt.[5] Hakluyt was a tireless investigator of all matters marine and he made it his business to know all the leading "players" of his day. He was also a leading advocate of English seafaring, exploration, overseas settlement and naval power. In the late 1580s he was completing his monumental work "The Principal Navigations of the English Nation" and he proposed to include in it a new world map of high quality produced by Edward Wright, a mathematician turned navigator and cartographer, who had established mathematically an exact method of constructing charts "on Mercator's Projection". Further, having been to sea on at least two ocean voyages, Wright understood the practical advantages, particularly that, on a Mercator chart, a desired course based on a compass bearing can be drawn as a straight line, a "rhumb line". Wright had also produced the mathematics ("A table of meridional parts") for converting a plane chart for presentation on a globe. In 1589 Hakluyt wrote in the preface to the first edition of the Principal Navigations that he had included in his work "one of the best generalle mappes of the world" (This was Edward Wright's world map of 1599) pending " the coming out of a very large and exact terrestriall Globe, collected and reformed according to the newest, secretest, and latest discoveries, both Spanish, Portugall, and English, composed by M. Emmerie Mollineux of Lambeth, a rare gentleman in his profession, being therein for divers years, greatly supported by the purse and liberalitie of the worshipful merchant M. William Sanderson". It looks very much as though Wright's map and Molyneux' globes were conceived in parallel, and this seems to be supported by the facts that (i) they both contained the same up-to-date information and (ii) Wright provided the mathematical basis for shaping the "gores" – the carefully cut pieces of paper, carrying the cartographical information, which were glued to the globe to present a seamless sphere. The third member of the Molyneux team was Jodocus Hondius, a skilful and innovative engraver, who as a protestant refugee from the Low Countries, lived and worked in London in the period 1583–93: he engraved the plates for printing the gores for the globes, and he went on to make maps and globes, including the Molyneux globes, later, back in the Netherlands. The fourth member was Sanderson, the merchant adventurer and patron who supplied the cash (over £1,000) and general support. Feeding the team with first hand knowledge of the latest information were commanders like Drake, Cavendish, Raleigh, and John Davis, and here, too, we can see the hand of Hakluyt, acting as liaison between the eminent naval men on the one hand and the academics and artisans on the other. In addition, there were specialist "consultants" offering ideas and advice like Dr.Dee, Thomas Harriot and Robert Hues (who wrote the manual for the use of the globes, the "Tractatus de Globis").

In this way, it is suggested, the Principal Navigations, Edward Wright's map and the Molyneux globes, all formed part of the Imperial Vision for English naval expansion, based in turn on the circumnavigations of Drake and Cavendish, the failure of the Armada and the emergence of England as a potential world force based on sea power.

The grand design would be crowned by identifying it with the Queen who had inspired resistance to the Armada and embodied the vision of seaborne expansion. The symbolic significance of the dedication of the Molyneux globes to the Queen, which seems to have been designed and written by Sanderson personally, with a latin version by his friend William Camden, the scholar and antiquary, was not lost upon her.[6]

Not much is known about Molyneux and no other globe or map is attributed to him – which makes his achievement that much more remarkable.[7] He was a mathematician and a precision engineer, making mathematical instruments, compasses and hourglasses. He also designed (and perhaps made) ordnance, for marine use: the Lord High Admiral was instructed to consult him[8] and in 1594 the Queen granted him, jointly with another, a present of £200 and a pension of £50 p.a. It has been established, however, that he had been to sea ("my own voyages") and sailed with Drake, and possibly Cavendish on his circumnavigation.[9] Thus, though his voyages have not been precisely defined, he would have experienced the practical problems of navigation, pilotage, keeping rutters, using navigational instruments and so on. His interest in navigational problems is underlined by Simon Forman's efforts to convince him that he (Forman) had a system for calculating longitude.[10] Molyneux's English pension ceased when he emigrated to Holland in 1597, perhaps to pursue sales of his globes to European customers. His new ideas for cannon were considered by the States General and protected by a 12 year patent, but Molyneux died young in 1598 and his widow was awarded a Netherlands government pension. Edward Wright was a Cambridge mathematician, who became a cartographer. As a young man he found time to sail with Drake to the West Indies in 1585–6, and thus met Thomas Harriot when Drake brought home the Roanoke settlers; and also on a privateering voyage to the Azores in 1589. On return he taught navigational mathematics in London and published "Certain Errors of Navigation". We have already mentioned how he built on Mercator's work,[11] having realised from his own experience at sea the vast superiority of charts drawn on Mercator's projection. He also produced the high quality world map in 1599 ("A true hydrographical description") which Hakluyt published with his Principal Navigations.[12] Jodocus Hondius was the original engraver of the plates for the Molyneux globes. He returned to the Netherlands in 1593 and took over the production of the Molyneux globes but he soon dropped them and turned to producing globes of his own, together with other charts and maps, building a prosperous business. John Davis suggests that he was instrumental in bringing Sanderson and Molyneux together, writing "Made by master Emery Mullneux, a man wel qualited, of a good judgment and very experte in many excellent practises in myself being the onely meane with master Sanderson to imploy Mulineux therein, whereby he is now growne to a most exquisite perfection". Davis also proudly states, in relation to his searches for the NW Passage, that the Molyneux terrestrial globes show "how far I proceeded and in what form this discovery lieth".[13]

Terrestrial globes had a number of functions.[14] First, they were intrinsically useful. They were superior to flat charts, in that they permanently portrayed the whole world, while charts had to be made in separate sheets which needed to be hung up to be studied and rolled up when not in use. If not too large they were portable and thus could be taken to sea.[15] The relative positions of distant places could be easily considered, together with the distances involved, the prevailing winds and currents, and the courses to be set to achieve a rhumb line or Great Circle course. Globes were invaluable, too, in teaching navigation since they made it easier to demonstrate the celestial triangle problems which had to be solved mathematically. This still has to be done to-day though computers do the work quickly and are unaffected by sea-sickness. Secondly, when mounted in wooden frames, a pair of terrestrial and celestial globes formed a decorative feature to grace the library or saloon of any monarch or magnate. Thirdly, globes had an important symbolic role in the 16th and 17th centuries, and are often seen in portraits.[16] Maps, too, in a smaller way, could play a symbolic role: the owner of a private estate, a principality or a kingdom who commissioned and displayed a map of his domain proclaimed his power and importance.

The Molyneux globes were larger than any predecessor, being about 2' 1" in diameter.[17] Smaller, cheaper versions were also made, in Robert Hues' words, "so that the meaner Students might herein also be provided for". The larger globes seem to have cost £20 for the pair and the smaller £2, but the overall cost could be increased if the globes were specially finished or ornamented and/or if freight to their destination had to be paid.[18] The globes incorporated technical advances. Molyneux used a new material to produce a smooth surface which was consistent with a true spherical shape and also resistant to changes in humidity, an important advantage at sea. According to one account this was "plaster",[19] according to another, flour paste.[20] Again there were innovations in the frame, so that the globe could be revolved smoothly. The celestial globes had limited new information but the terrestrial ones had a wealth of up-to-date and accurate details, for example the Roanoke settlements organised by Raleigh (1586–90) and the voyages of John Davis searching for the NW Passage in 1585, 1586 and 1587. The overall construction and the delineation of the features on the globe (Hondius was an outstanding and innovative engraver) were aesthetically pleasing. The first terrestrial globe presented to the Queen (end-July 1591) had a canopy or circular curtain suspended above it, which could be opened or closed, perhaps to protect the globe from dust or sunlight, or merely to embellish it: this feature is found on some other early globes,[21] though one scholar suggests that the cover was to conceal the details on the globe from unauthorised eyes [22]

As a result of these characteristics the Molyneux globes were immediately recognised as the best available – an amazing achievement considering that they were the first globes made in England and the largest ever at that date. The globes did however have one commercial defect which would have had to be corrected if they were to be sold internationally. While it seems that foreign sales were intended, very few actually took place and there appears not to have been any systematic selling. The dedication to Queen Elizabeth, and the symbolic claim or invitation to global domination through England sea power, would have been a serious deterrent in European markets (and would have required a separate "edition").

From Hakluyt's promotional mention in his Preface in the Principal Navigations in 1589 it sounds as though the project was by that year already well advanced, with the financier in place: Sanderson was to invest over £1000. The first completed globe (a terrestrial one) was presented to Queen Elizabeth at Greenwich at the end of July 1591 by Molyneux. Prior to that event there were two interesting visitors to Molyneux's workshop in Lambeth – Dr Simon Forman and Petruccio Ubaldini. Forman was a well known physician, usually, but quite unfairly, probably as a result of professional jealousy, described as "a quack doctor".[23] He visited Molyneux on 10th April 1591 and observed that he cast true spheres for the globes by coating them with flour paste, this material being resistant to humidity changes – a useful innovation.[24] Forman also offered Molyneux a method of determining longitude, but did not, apparently, follow this up.[25] Ubaldini visited Molyneux probably around the same time (on several occasions) and provided important detailed information about the globes and the plans for marketing them.[26] Ubaldini was an Italian who had settled in England in 1562 and was well known at the Court. His account of the globes, based on these visits to Molyneux' workshop and his leisurely inspection of the terrestrial globe presented to the Queen in July 1591, were carefully written down in August 1591 and sent to one Francesco Parola (an employee of the Grand Duke of Tuscany) visiting London, who had accompanied Ubaldini on one of the workshop visits. This letter was intended as an aide-memoire to remind Parola of what he had seen, and to be handed on to the Grand Duke; since Ubaldini and Parola had in mind to secure Molyneux globes for the Grand Duke. The descriptive letter was discovered only recently in the State Archives in Florence. Uboldini's fascinating description can be read, translated into English, in the Crino/Wallis article. In writing to Parola, Uboldini said "I had seen these globes of his before he issued a single one, and liked them very much, but the first completed globe was to be the Queen's and he was still working on it". This underlines the slow, painstaking nature of the work.

Uboldini also had some interesting things to say about Molyneux and about the marketing plans for the globes. "Although he is of very humble origin and has no other language[27] he betrays a strong desire to make himself known abroad for these globes of his and takes down the names of several princes, both Italian and German, intending to present his work in person…But it must be remembered that the Dedication to the Queen has to be printed with the royal arms and its wording suggests that he gave her the globe to let her see at a glance how much of the seas she could control by means of her naval forces." The underlying symbolism was as obvious to Uboldini as to the Queen herself. It is interesting to speculate whether Sanderson, as a merchant with long experience of European markets, had also spotted the marketing faux pas, and whether he was similarly committed to the secondary market in Europe. Clearly his main motive in the Molyneux project was patriotic, and it is reasonable to assume that, as with the backing of John Davis, realising a profit was secondary. Since he was an experienced commercial man, he may have been relaxed about the need to alter or replace the copper plates for "an export version" Certainly the plates had to be re-engraved later to accommodate additional geographical material. In the event, based on the globes which have survived, there were at least two German customers: it is not known whether these sales were made by Molyneux or Hondius or which version of the terrestrial globe was involved. It may be noted that the text on the globes was in latin, still a universal language in Europe, as was the "official handbook" or manual, the Tractatus de Globis published by Robert Hues.

We move on to the end of July 1591 when Molyneux presented the first terrestrial globe to the Queen.at Greenwich. Uboldini was present and had, in addition, seen it "at my leisure when it was taken there". He describes the canopy or circular curtain, concluding "truly it is an object worthy of a prince": clearly he considered the canopy as a decorative feature.[28] Sanderson also had his day, or rather two days, of glory a little later, probably in 1592. The Queen honoured him with two separate visits to his house at Newington Butts, and produced two characteristic, Elizabethan witticisms in her words of thanks. Sir William in An Answer reports: The Terrestrial being first presented to Queen Elizabeth, at an entertainment at my father's house (then Newington Butts) upon which she was pleased to descant 'The whole earth, a present for a Prince; but with the Spanish King's leave[29] in speed upon the Globe of the Earth: his fore-feet over-reaching, with this Motto, "Non sufficit Orbis " (The world is too small for me). The symbolic significance, that the globe conferred or suggested world authority, was obvious and, no doubt, pleasing to Elizabeth. Sir William continues: At her second entertainment there, she receiving the Celestial said , "Thou hast presented me with the Heavens also: God guide me, so to Govern my part of the one, that I may enjoy but a mansion place in the other "[30] It was probably on one or other of these occasions, that the Queen instructed Sanderson to "advance the bearing of his crest, antiently the Talbot, and his Motto, 'Rien Sans Dieu', with the addition of a Globe Terrestrial, affixed to the Sun in lustre, proper, with this Motto, 'Opera Mundi', to him and his heires for ever".

Shortly afterwards, probably in 1594, Sanderson visited the College of Heralds to have the crest of his coat of arms "enhanced" and a new motto added, as Queen Elizabeth had directed: the case was handled by the Garter King of Arms, Dethick. This would have involved the checking of the existing arms and of the "quartering" which reflected the family's earlier alliances. The whole exercise seems to have produced some mirth among the snobbish heralds who apparently thought the Sandersons "mean" and pretentious.[31] The pedigree of the Sandersons produced by the Heralds and still held by the College[32] seems to be somewhat later, since the most recent event recorded is dated 1621.

Sanderson's arms, enhanced on
the Queen's instructions

Later Molyneux globes, and some of John Norden's English county maps.[33] display the advanced or enhanced Sanderson arms.[34] There is no record of Sanderson's descendants heirs ever using them, but it is hard to imagine Sir William failing to do so.

While the Molyneux globes were universally acclaimed we do not know whether the project was commercially successful or at least recovered its costs, and the globes did not in the event stay in production long. Contemporary comments, however, suggest a fairly wide distribution[35] Molyneux emigrated to the Netherlands in 1597, possibly with a view to selling the globes in Europe. It is interesting to consider Sanderson's reaction to this development. Presumably, as the patron "who made it all happen", he had some say, but once the transfer had taken place, this would be gone. With the two key players and the plates being removed, there were unlikely to be many more sales in England.[36] Had everything remained in England the globes might have enjoyed a long life, particularly in the absence of competition, (very different from the Low Countries) with updates as necessary, and ongoing glory for Sanderson.[37] Perhaps Sanderson was satisfied with getting the globes published and winning the approval of the Queen, without being too much concerned with the longer term. He may even have encouraged Molyneux to try his luck in the European market. The whole operation, including the plates, was handed over to Hondius, who had returned to Amsterdam in 1593: perhaps the idea was that Molyneux would devote himself to sales and marketing (though, as we have noted, he had no languages other than English), while Hondius concentrated on the design and manufacture. Molyneux did interest the States General in his marine ordnance – he was granted a patent – but he died shortly afterwards (1598), and the Netherlands Government granted a pension to his widow.

After an initial spurt of activity Hondius apparently did not support the Molyneux globes for long. He added much new material up to around 1597[38] and in the same year he published a Dutch translation of Hues' *Tractatus de Globis*; but in 1597 he also started work on his own, somewhat smaller, globes, with a diameter around 14", publishing them from 1600. Hondius' plans were challenged by competitors in the Netherlands courts, but, since he built a very successful cartography business, we may assume that it was for commercial reasons that he dropped the Molyneux globes and opted for a smaller globe published under his own name. It is difficult to avoid the impression that the larger Molyneux globes at perhaps £20 per pair plus freight, together with additional costs of embellishing and installing, were aimed at institutions and very rich individuals – a limited market, with probably only a small gross margin: Hondius' new globes sound like an improved version of Molyneux' smaller globes.

To-day three celestial and two terrestrial Molyneux globes survive, all in the larger size, as follows:- (i) the Middle Temple pair. The terrestrial is dated 1603: the plate has been changed from 1592, while the celestial is dated 1592.[39] These were given (or bequeathed) to the Society by William Crashawe, who was Preacher to the Middle and Inner Temples (1605–1613) and a prodigious collector, mainly of books. It is not known whether Crashawe acquired the globes, which he described as "one of the fairest paire of globes in England" directly from Molyneux/Hondius or "second hand" from someone else. The terrestrial globe includes new information up to about 1597, for example, Ralegh's discoveries in "Guiana": they are thus from a "second" or "later" edition, produced in the Netherlands.[40] (ii) the Petworth House terrestrial globe, discovered by Helen Wallis in 1949. This came from the Tower of London where it was owned by the 9th Earl of Northumberland, having, according to family tradition, been a gift to him from his fellow prisoner Ralegh. It is dated 1592 and, as at that time Sanderson and Raleigh were working closely together, it was probably one of the first globes to be completed after those destined for the Queen. Almost certainly, therefore, it may be allocated to the "first" or original edition. This globe, incidentally, has suffered from wear and tear and has been repaired in modern times: no doubt it was much used in the Tower. (iii) A celestial globe in the Hessiches Landesmuseum at Kassel, apparently derived from the collection of Landgrave William IV of Hesse; although, since he died in 1592, it may have been acquired by his son.[41] In 1921 a pair was recorded but it seems that the terrestrial globe was destroyed in WW II.[42] This globe is from 1592 or 1593[43] (iv) A celestial globe in the Germanisches National Museum at Nuremberg. Its structure differs from that of the Petworth terrestrial globe. It was recorded as a Hondius globe. It looks, therefore, as though these German survivors were from an edition earlier than the Petworth globe, but not necessarily from the "original" edition. It would be pleasing to think that these European sales may have been made by Molyneux himself after he emigrated to the Netherlands, in the short period before his death.

In addition to these survivors there is specific evidence of sales or gifts of additional Molyneux globes, as follows:- (i) Sanderson presented Molyneux globes (presumably pairs) to the Universities of Oxford and Cambridge[44] (ii) Sir Thomas Bodley purchased a pair for his library (iii) the Warden of All Souls, Dr Robert Hovenden, purchased a pair for the College (iv) Sanderson presented a terrestrial globe (in the smaller size) in 1595 to Lord Salisbury, together with a manual, probably Robert Hues' Tractatus de Globis"[45] (v) Thomas Laughton, a Cambridge graduate who was appointed public preacher at St.Mary's, Shrewsbury in 1592 gave a Molyneux globe as an "inaugural gift" to the library of Shrewsbury School. It was probably a terrestrial one. (vi) Sir William in An Answer states that Sanderson presented to Prince Henry "that then admired double Sphear....with a Manuscript of the use thereof", but it seems unlikely that this refers to a pair of the smaller Molyneux globes and Hues' manual for their use. This gift to Prince Henry was probably of an armillary sphere[46] (vii) There is also general evidence as to the distribution of the globes. Thomas Hood stated, through the character of his pupil, "They are now in the hands of many with whom I have to deal";[47] and over 60 years later, in 1656, Sir William, in An Answer, was able to say of the Molyneux globes "They are yet in being, great and small ones, Celestiall and Terrestriall, in both our Universities, and in severall Libraries (here, and beyond Seas)".

In addition, the existence and importance of the Molyneux globes, and of Edward Wright's world map of 1599, entered the consciousness of the general public. In Shakespeare's Comedy of Errors (1594)[48] Dromio and Antipholus are discussing, in somewhat indelicate terms, the former's wooer, Nell, "the kitchen wench". Antipholus asks "Then she bears some breadth?" and Dromio replies, "No longer from head to foot than from hip to hip: she is spherical like a globe; and I could find out countries in her".

It is perhaps significant that this reference to a globe, followed by a catalogue of countries, is not in the "serious" verse but in the vulgar, "low" dialogue crafted for the groundlings. In Shakespeare's, Twelfth Night (1601),[49] again in a comic dialogue, there are two interesting cartographical references, "You are now sailed into the north of my lady's opinion; where you will hang like an icicle on a Dutchman's beard", and "He does smile his face into more lines than there are in the new map with the augmentation of the Indies". The first of these two quotation is usually regarded as an echo of the voyage by Willem Barentsz to Novya-Zemlya, which was recorded in the "second edition" of the terrestrial globes, while the second appears to refer to Edward Wright's world map of 1599:[50]Thomas Dekker, in The Gull's Hornbook (1609)[51] writes, "What an excellent workman, therefore, were he that could cast the globe of it into a new mould. And not to make it look like Mullineux his globe, with a round face sleeked and washed over with whites of eggs, but to have it plano as it was at first, with all the circles, lines, parallels and figures".

The importance of the Molyneux globes, as efficient aids to astronomy, navigation and so on, is underlined by the four books describing them and their applications which were produced shortly after their publication in 1592. (i) The first was a manual for the use of the globes published in 1592 and written by Thomas Hood of Trinity College, Cambridge, who was a "mathematical lecturer" at Sir Thomas Smythe's house in Philpot Lane in the City.[52] (ii) In 1594 Robert Hues, originally a classical scholar but switching later to geography, mathematics and navigation, published his Tractatus de Globis.[53] He had experience at sea, sailing with Cavendish on his second, disastrous voyage, and returning to England about the time that the globes were first published i.e 1592. His work appears to have been recognised as the "official manual" and it went through several editions. The Tractatus appears to be the manual that Sanderson sent (with a smaller terrestrial globe) to Lord Salisbury in 1595, and, significantly, Hondius published a Dutch translation of it in 1597. Hues, like Thomas Harriot, became a "gentleman pensioner" of the 9th Earl of Northumberland, and he was one of Ralegh's executors. He had dedicated his Tractatus to Ralegh. It was at one time thought that the treatise on rhumb lines included in Hues' Tractatus de Globis was the work of Thomas Harriot, but this view has been abandoned and this treatise is now recognised as by Hues himself.[54] (iii) The fullest description is in "M. Blundrevile his Exercises, Containing Six Treatises" published in 1594, with a later edition in 1597. (iv) It appears that Molyneux himself published "The Globes Celestial and Terrestrial Set Forth in plano" in 1592 but no copy seems to have survived.

In this way the English Globe phenomenon, without either antecedent or successor, was all over in twelve years. While Sanderson was known to and occasionally employed by Government, and consulted on economic matters, and attracted a wider reputation with his support of John Davis' expeditions and Raleigh's activities, his patronage of the Molyneux globes, with the symbolic presentations to the Queen, ranks as his main claim to fame in Elizabeth's reign.

Part Three
Trust Betrayed and an
Obstinate Loyalty

11

South America: the Search for El Dorado

Reverting to a chronological approach, we may describe Ralegh's secret marriage. This took place on 19th November 1591, the date being established only in the 20th century following the discovery of the diary of Sir Arthur Throckmorton, Bess Throckmorton's elder brother and guardian. A baby boy, Damarel, was born about four months later and christened on 10th April 1592 but it seems that he died in infancy, since no further reference to him occurs. Knowing that his secret marriage to a maid of honour, with whom he had been conductng an affair and who was already pregnant, would outrage and infuriate the Queen, Ralegh deliberately denied the marriage to Salisbury, in hope that, by the time the truth emerged, he would have achieved some naval glory, which might soften the blow. Ralegh had totally miscalculated the Queen's reaction – by early August 1592 he and Bess were both in the Tower.

Ironically, some naval glory was indeed achieved, and it was due to Ralegh's foresight, but it did not shield him from the Queen's fury – though the treasure captured in the naval action served as a "ransom" to secure the release of Ralegh and Bess from the Tower. In January 1592, before the marriage story broke, Ralegh was given command of a major expedition to Panama, composed partly of Royal Navy ships, partly privately owned (Ralegh himself, his brother Carew and the Earl of Cumberland contributed ships) and partly City of London armed merchantmen, some sixteen vessels in all. In the same month Ralegh received from the Queen a 99 year lease of the Sherborne estate, which he later enlarged to a freehold. Ralegh invested in the voyage, with the assistance of Sanderson, as did the Queen The fleet eventually sailed in May, with Ralegh instructed by the Queen to return, handing over command to Frobisher. On intelligence received, however, Ralegh changed the plan, dividing the fleet between Frobisher, who was sent to hover off the Spanish coast, and Sir John Borough who was sent to sail towards the Azores. Borough captured an enormous, richly laden, Portuguese carrack on her way home from the East Indies, the Madre de Dios, which was eventually brought into Dartmouth in September 1592. Looting and plundering broke out on a massive scale; and Raleigh was released from the Tower to restore order and attempt a controlled management of the booty. The "Commission for Sale of Prizes taken by Sir Walter Raleigh's Fleet", dated 30th October 1592, provided how the various interested parties would be represented "William Sanderson, merchant, for Sir Walter Raleigh, and for the captains, masters, gentlemen, soldiers, mariners and fellows in the said voyage."[1] The division of spoils was somewhat uneven – the Queen took the lion's share, some £80,000; Cumberland got a profit of £17,000 on £19,000 invested; the city merchants £12,000 on £6,000 invested, while Raleigh and his associates got only £2,000 on £34, 000 invested. This represented a loss to Ralegh as some money had been borrowed and interest had to be paid. Raleigh was disappointed, but could hardly complain, and clearly realised that this was the "ransom" he had to pay to buy himself and Bess out of the Tower:[2] He and Bess were released in December 1592 and retired to Sherborne. Raleigh was re-admitted to Court five years later in 1597, but Bess never was.

In 1593 and 1594 Raleigh was based at Sherborne, though he was elected MP for Mitchell in North Cornwall in 1593 and was active in Parliament. During this time the Sherborne estate was developed. Ralegh's original plan was to restore the old castle, but this was abandoned by 1594 and, instead, the "new castle", originally known as "Sherborne Lodge", was built on the site of the old hunting lodge of the Bishop of Salisbury. It was rectangular, four stories high, with large square-headed windows filled with diamond pane glass and the house was rendered in the latest fashion. Sherborne Lodge and the estate were much admired. John Aubrey remarked "He built a delicate lodge in the park not big but very convenient for the bigness....In short and indeed 'tis a sweet and pleasant place and site as any in the West, perhaps none like it".[3] Ralegh had realised his long held ambition – a "seat" worthy of his importance which was at the same time innovative, elegant and comfortable, with a touch of fantasy. There remain many features in the enlarged building providing a direct link with Ralegh's design and domestic arrangements. In 1600 Ralegh added hexagonal turrets to the four corners topped with heraldic beasts.[4]

The family lost Sherborne on Ralegh's conviction for treason and attainder, and James I granted the estate to Sir John Digby in 1617 on his retirement as English ambassador to Madrid. The Castle (as it has come to be called) and the estate have remained in the hands of the Wingfield Digby family to the present day.

Raleigh's half brother Adrian Gilbert carried out landscaping and built

The Fireplace in Ralegh's Study

the water-gardens, spending some £700; and when he eventually sued Ralegh his claim was rejected as "stale". It is thought that the substantial costs of enhancing the Sherborne estate, perhaps some £10,000, were underpinned by cash from the Babbington estates, forfeited to the Crown and given to Ralegh by the Queen in 1587.

The failure of the Roanoke settlement (the final English visit when no survivors were found took place in 1590) did not dampen Ralegh's enthusiasm for America, though he now switched his attention to the South Atlantic – the area around the Orinoco River. This change of heart had been developing at least since 1586 when Ralegh's privateering raid to the Azores produced a valuable Spanish prisoner, Sarmiento, the Governor of Patagonia. He lived for some time with Ralegh in Durham House and fed him stories of the wealth of the Spanish Empire. As a result, Ralegh's

The chief is coated with gold dust

restless aspirations, combining English imperial expansion with the acquisition of power and wealth for himself, linked, at this stage, with re-establishing himself in Elizabeth's eyes, transferred to South America. His thinking focussed on (i) spoiling the Spanish (ii) founding a colony, with the English befriending the native population against the Spanish and (iii) procuring precious stones, pearls and, above all, gold. The specific objective was the real or mythical "golden city" known by the local Indians as Manoa and by the Spanish as El Dorado, "the golden one": El Dorado was originally the description of the King of the city who was supposed to be coated with gold dust on ceremonial occasions.

El Dorado[5]

The point of departure for the El Dorado story is, almost certainly, Lake Guatavita thought to have been created by a meteorite fall near Bogota in Colombia, at an altitude of 10,000 feet. The area around the lake was inhabited by the Chibchas. In 1539 three Spanish expeditions, launched from Venezuela, Colombia and Ecuador, independently searching for gold and emeralds, converged on Lake Guadavita, stole all the treasure that they could find and, effectively, wiped out the Chibchas. The leader of the Colombian expedition was Gonzalo Jimenez de Quesada. He was eventually rewarded, when almost 70 years of age, by being appointed Governor of the Province of El Dorado (stretching from Colombia in the west to the Atlantic coast facing Trinidad). By his will, in 1579, he nominated as his successor his niece Maria – who was the wife of the Spanish army officer Antonio de Berrio.[6]

The Spanish were told of the custom by which the chief of the Chibchas, on his accession, was put out onto the Lake on a balsa raft with his lieutenants and they sacrificed gold and other treasure to placate the spirit or god of the Lake. The chief was naked but covered in gold dust, which he washd off in the Lake.[7] Certainly, the Spanish recovered gold and other valuables from the Lake, in particular in 1578 when Antonio Sepulveda caused a cutting to be made at one point in the Lake's rim to lower the depth.

The reports of these events which circulated were or became distorted. First, it was wrongly believed that the plentiful gold came from the Guadavita area. In fact, it was the proceeds, accumulated over many years of prosperous trading in salt by the Chibchas; so that when the tribe was wiped out there was no ongoing source of gold to be exploited.

Secondly, it was reported that there was a Golden City.(so that "El Dorado" was transferred from describing the King or chief to describing

Balsa raft modelled in gold (in the Gold Museum, Bogota)

their city) In fact, the Chibchas lived in villages and Bogota was only founded by the Spanish (as Santa Fe de Bogota) in 1539. Thirdly, a number of "gold" artefacts were found to be, not gold, but gilded copper. The Chibchas operated a copper mine and were accomplished metalworkers.

In this way a larger myth was built around the established facts, but, in addition, the supposed site of El Dorado migrated over 1000 miles eastwards from Colombia to the area between the Orinoco and Amazon Rivers. The reason for this is not altogether clear.[9]

The El Dorado story thus focussed Ralegh's interest on the area south of the Orinoco River and one of the reconnaissance expeditions which Ralegh sent out in 1594 seemed to provide some documentary evidence of gold.

When Ralegh captured Antonio de Berrio in Trinidad in 1595 and persuaded him to talk about his own extensive searches for El Dorado his enthusiasm must have been re-doubled – he seems, too, to have caught the "gold fever" from Berrio (and indeed retained the infection for the rest of his life). The many months which Berrio had spent, in three separate expeditions,[10] ranging between the Orinoco delta and Colombia dwarfed the four weeks in which Ralegh travelled some 200 miles on the Orinoco; but this, and Berrio's attempts to dissuade him, did nothing to modify Ralegh's convictions.

Ralegh lobbied in London for permission to mount an expedition and Sanderson worked on the finance. In 1594 Ralegh sent out two

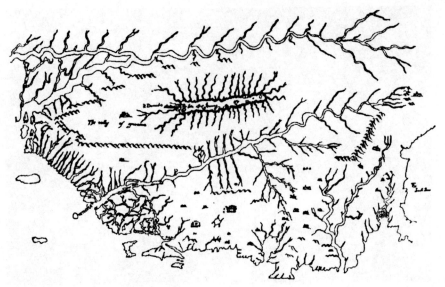

Sketch of Ralegh's map of Guyana in the British Library. The map is "upside down". The Amazon and Orinoco Rivers are accurately presented but the "centipede lake", with El Dorado at the left i.e. eastern, end is imaginary.

reconnaissance parties under John Borough and Jacob Whiddon, and by the end of that year a fleet of five ships, provisioned for a year, with some 150 men, was being assembled at Plymouth.

During the previous ten years of his collaboration with Sanderson, Ralegh had been prevented by the Queen from going abroad. Once the Manoa/El Dorado expedition had been decided on, to be led by Ralegh in person, Sanderson reckoned that he should seek a settlement of accounts and obtain a release from Ralegh, to avoid any come-back from his executors or creditors if he was killed in the course of the voyage. Sanderson attempted to bring this about but, over some months, Ralegh was evasive and kept asking for more details. In the light of subsequent events, it seems likely that Ralegh was hoping, by avoiding a settlement, to "keep him on a string" for use in the future. However, when it became time for him to leave for Plymouth to embark, Ralegh invited Sanderson to ride down with him and help him with the final preparations for putting to sea. This provided the opportunity for Sanderson to press his point.

We now describe what happened in the days leading up to the point where the two men parted in anger late at night a few hours before Raleigh sailed off to South America: this was in January-February 1595. When they reached Devon it looks as though Ralegh lodged with his friend Sir Christopher Harris, who lived at Plymstock, some three miles out of

Plymouth[11] and Sanderson was accommodated nearby. After a few days the accounts which Sanderson had supplied, backed-up with receipts, cancelled bonds and other supporting documentation, were "audited" by Thomas Harriot, Ralegh's polymath "chief of staff", and a deed of release was signed by Ralegh, witnessed by Christopher Harris and John Meere (Ralegh's steward or bailiff at Sherborne) and handed to Sanderson. The accounts showed that there was a small sum outstanding due from Ralegh to Sanderson.

A few days later, apparently at the suggestion of his wife Bess, Ralegh asked Sanderson, in turn, to execute a release to him, so that Sanderson could make no subsequent claims against his estate or Bess if he (Ralegh) died in the course of the voyage. Sanderson agreed to this but excepted out of the release some £1,600 or £1,700 which he (Sanderson) had recently borrowed on his own credit and handed over to Ralegh.towards the cost of the planned expedition. Sanderson was thus liable to his lender both to repay the capital sum and, in the meantime, to pay running interest. So far, so good – these sensible commercial arrangements appear to have been completed in an amicable manner, despite Ralegh's earlier evasions.

A few days later again, a dramatic change occurred, in Sanderson's own words.[12] "At the very instant upon his departure in his sayd intended voyage in the night time, under pretence he had to see the sayd Release so made by him, which was sealed and delivered many dayes before unto your sayd subject as aforesaid; and your sayd subject nothing doubting of any ill meaning of his the sayd Sir Walter Ralegh gave the sayd release unto the sayd Sir Walter Raleghes hands who perusing the same a while gave the sayd release unto the sayd Thomas Herriots willing him not to deliver the same to your sayd subject unless he the sayd Sir Walter Ralegh should miscarry in his sayd voyage; but yf he should returne then to give it to himself againe with many more words to the same effect..." Ralegh also said that in his absence Sanderson might "borrow" the release from Harriot to show to his creditors but must then return it to Harriot. Not surprisingly, Sanderson was outraged at Ralegh's behaviour, "And so your subject being much grieved and discontented at his wicked doings turned from him without wishing or bidding him farewell the same being at the very instant of his departure and at midnight as he was about to take shipping as aforesaid".

This account is based on Sanderson's recollection, some sixteen years later, when Raleigh and his "administrators", appointed to manage his personal property following his attainder in 1603, sued Sanderson in the Chancery Court in 1611, demanding that Sanderson re-account for £60,000 of the cash transactions which he had handled on Ralegh's behalf in the years prior to 1595. Sanderson had to defend himself and mount a counterclaim, after having all his evidence confiscated, since all the vouchers, receipts, discharged bills and so on were attached to the release document which Ralegh had taken back by a trick and handed to Harriot. No attempt was made by Raleigh's team in the litigation sixteen years later to challenge the account of what happened in January-February 1595, though there was some sniping on details, which will be noticed as it occurs. In fact, the case presented in Court on Ralegh's behalf by his administrators confimed Sanderson's recollection of what had occurred in 1595 since they, effectively, said, "Yes, Ralegh did grant Sanderson a release, but it was conditional, not absolute, and all parties agreed to this at the time, and therefore Sanderson is now liable to re-account for everything down to 1595".

What really upset Sanderson, as appears from the documentation in the litigation over 16 years later, was

(i)   what he regarded as Ralegh's dishonesty in recovering by a trick the formal release document (with all the supporting evidence)

(ii) Ralegh trying to impose unilaterally and retrospectively conditions on the formal release document, which had been duly "signed, sealed and delivered" i.e. was absolute and unconditional in its terms, if he (Ralegh) survived and returned – namely an obligation to re-account all over again for all the earlier transactions. These went back at least some eight years prior to 1595.[13]

(iii) that by getting back the formal release document by a trick Ralegh had in addition deprived Sanderson of all the evidence supporting the accounts which he had presented, for example, the signed receipts for money which Sanderson had disbursed on Ralegh's behalf; since all the "supporting documents" were attached to the deed of release.

(iv) the fact that he had managed over ten years, without any reward or remuneration, and without any criticism or complaint, to keep Raleigh's affairs afloat and solvent

(v)   the fact that over the same period he (Sanderson) had brought in at least £30,000 (around £4 million to-day) which Ralegh would never have been able to raise on his own credit.

It must therefore be emphasised that Sanderson's anger and withdrawal without wishing Ralegh farewell on the voyage was not primarily about money. When he accompanied Ralegh to Plymouth (at Ralegh's invitation) and indeed up to Ralegh's trickery on the night of his departure, there had been no suggestion that Sanderson should cease to be his "honorary treasurer". The mutual releases were not to terminate their collaboration but (i) to establish the exact financial position between the parties, and (ii) to protect Sanderson, Ralegh and his estate, and Bess, *in respect of transactions up to that point in time,* in case Ralegh failed to return. "Settling accounts" in this way is normal practice between partners, a principal and his banker, a principal and his treasurer and so on where, for example, a defined transaction has been completed or where, as here, one party is about to risk his life. It is equally normal practice after accounts have been settled, for the balance to be paid off by the party owing money to the other party, either at once or gradually as the balance of debt swings back in the opposite direction. No doubt this had happened before during the 10 years or so when the men had worked together.

Sanderson's sadness and anger were based rather on ingratitude and betrayal of trust.

When Sanderson stormed off into the night it de facto terminated the treasurership. We do not know whether Ralegh and his advisers either then (Ralegh went straight to his ship so there was little time) or subsequently took any legal steps or simply regarded Sanderson as having resigned. In due course Harriot took over the cash and accounting responsibilities, while John Shelbury became Ralegh's representative with regard to the wine licences and the export of undyed cloth. In these circumstances what was to be done about the money owed by Ralegh to Sanderson?

Why did Ralegh "wickedly" seize back the release and attempt retrospectively to convert its absolute terms into conditional ones? We have discussed at the outset of their relationship the critical difference in rank between the two men and also the mutual advantages for them of adding a banking or treasurership dimension to what had commenced simply as kinship by marriage. Since they had, for some 11 years, enjoyed a successful commercial collaboration, as well as a pleasant social relationship between the two married couples, it seems unlikely (though of course not impossible) that differences of rank, or a hitherto suppressed contempt for "trade", triggered Ralegh's high-handed action after this lapse of time. The steps which Ralegh actually took to try to undermine the effect of a signed and sealed document suggest a sharp, but not very learned, lawyer – which points to Ralegh's legal team – John Shelbury, Ralegh's solicitor and John Meere, the Sherborne steward who had some legal knowledge or qualification. As will appear later, they did not enjoy a high reputation, and Meere had been in prison for clipping coins and had forged Ralegh's signature on at least one occasion.

A possible explanation is as follows:- After several months of putting off Sanderson's request for a release, Ralegh invited him to accompany him to Plymouth. His legal team may have advised that there will be no harm in granting Sanderson a release, "because you can then in turn ask him for a release which will protect you, your estate, your sons and Lady Ralegh". At the same time, they may have overlooked that Sanderson would insist that the £1,600 or £1,700 which he had raised on his own credit by borrowing from a third party (for the El Dorado expedition) must be "excepted" out of the release. Once the absolute releases had been exchanged, the slate would have been wiped clean – *except for the money owed to Sanderson,* and this would be payable sooner or later whether or not the Manao/El Dorado expedition was successful. In legal terminology the parties had "settled their accounts". If, on the other hand, there were still unsettled accounts, and Sanderson sued for the money owed to him, Ralegh could go to the Chancery Court and demand (i) that Sanderson should re-submit his accounts for approval (ii) that his claim to recover what he was owed should be stayed i.e. held up, until his accounts has been passed. There would then be the possibility of arguing over the accounts, "muddying the waters", running up costs, delaying matters and so on, which would certainly put off, and might perhaps finally smother, the claim to recover the money owed. It looks as though Ralegh's lawyer John Shelbury suddenly realised that by allowing the parties to exchange absolute releases he had thrown away this tactical advantage – and left his master in an exposed position.[14] This is why the shabby plan was hatched to try to convert retrospectively the absolute release which Ralegh had given Sanderson into a conditional release. At Plympton Ralegh laid down retrospective "decrees": sixteen years later an endorsement on Ralegh's absolute release document was forged to try to make it conditional.

Whatever prompted Ralegh's launch into what looks like sharp practice at the least, he must have taken a view on Sanderson's reaction to his attempt unilaterally to re-write a signed and sealed release. Ralegh displayed poor judgment of people on many occasions, for example, falling out quite unnecessarily with Lord Henry Howard, who poisoned James I against him 20 years later; antagonising Lord Deputy Fitzwilliam in Ireland; hiring John Meere out of prison to be the steward at Sherborne; misjudging the Queen' reaction over his affair and marriage with Bess Throckmorton; convincing himself that he had made a friend of Salisbury; acting disrespectfully to James I on first meeting him; plotting indiscreetly with Cobham. The best immediate outcome for Ralegh's ploy would have been for Sanderson to knuckle down and defer to Ralegh's personality and rank, accept the watering-down of the release and accept that he might have to wait for his money. Possibly this is what he thought would happen, overlooking the fact that to a leading City merchant misrepresentation and unfair dealing are as damning as cowardice to a military man or "conduct unbecoming" to a gentleman. However, if that was his expectation, while the short-term chances of avoiding a debt of some £1,700 would be improved, there could be no ongoing mutual trust.

An alternative explanation might be that Ralegh had come to "take Sanderson's contribution for granted", regarding him as "expendable" (echoes of Frobisher and Michael Lock) and was indifferent to his reaction.

It is difficult to see any way in which the principal/treasurer relationship could survive Ralegh's actions, so the only conclusions are (i) that he thought Sanderson's sacrifice was worth the chance of saving £1,700 or (ii) he totally misjudged the reaction of a leading merchant to his lawyer's shabby plan.

What was Ralegh seeking to achieve? The most likely answers are :- (a) to keep Sanderson "on a string" so that he would be "available" later i.e the same explanation as was offered to explain Ralegh's earlier evasions over giving a release at all (b) to provide a weapon for a pre-emptive strike to discourage Sanderson from seeking to recover by going to law the debts owed to him. Ralegh may not have been able to raise such a sum immediately, though at the time his annual income seems to have been around £8,000 –£10,000[15] so he could have paid what he owed, either at once or over a short period; but it seems pretty clear from looking at the figures that Ralegh deliberately chose not to pay. After 1603 the position changed, for the worse, when James I stripped Ralegh of his royal perquisites. Ralegh's plan evidently was (i) promises and honeyed words whenever the two men met (the Hounslow Heath meeting illustrates this) and (ii) launch a pre-emptive strike if Sanderson shows signs of commencing proceedings.

An interesting aspect of the unhappy evening at Plympton is the likely reaction of the others present – Lady Ralegh, Christopher Harris and Thomas Harriot. Lady Ralegh was, by all accounts, devoted to Ralegh but she was an exceptionally independent woman and could hardly have been comfortable witnessing the mistreatment of someone who had served her husband faithfully (and without any payment) for 10 years or so and who, with his wife, had supported and entertained her and her husband in the time of their disgrace and banishment from Court.

Christopher Harris was a friend of Ralegh's.[16] He was knighted later and there no reason to think that he was other than honest. Certainly Sanderson thought so, since in the litigation 16 years later he sought to obtain evidence from him on oath as to exactly what had happened in his house at Plympton 16 years earlier. Unfortunately Harris died before his evidence could be taken.

Harriot was a loyal servant of Ralegh and he has always been regarded as a honest, unambitious, apolitical, intellectual. He had been acquainted with Sanderson for some years, possibly ten, and they must have cooperated on a number of matters, for example establishing Ralegh's Munster estates as well as routine cash management. By agreement he had carried out a detailed audit of all Sanderson's records on Ralegh's behalf, asking many questions, and his approval must have been the basis of the formal release to Sanderson. He cannot fail to have been embarrassed (to put it no higher) to hear his master say that (i) all Sanderson's transactions would have to be re-justified *in certain circumstances which had no connection with the accuracy or otherwise of the accounts* which he had examined and approved only a few days earlier.(ii) if Sanderson wanted to show the release to his creditors (the release which, couched in absolute terms, had been handed to him by Ralegh a few days before) he, Sanderson, a leading City merchant, would have to ask the permission of Ralegh's servant, the much younger Harriot, to "borrow" the release and then return it afterwards.

It seems quite likely, therefore, that the Plympton Incident marked the point at which Harriot "modified" his loyalty to Ralegh – in that he either "looked for" or "responded to" the overtures of the Earl of Northumberland to become his "gentleman pensioner". Dr Shirley[17] reckons that "In the early 1590s, while Ralegh's life was in constant turmoil, Harriot began to look for a more secure patronage". Dr Shirley based this judgment on detailed analysis of how frequently Harriot dined with the Earl without Ralegh being present. Dr Shirley goes on to say, "Undoubtedly, it was during the seven months from February to September 1595, when Ralegh was pursuing his chimerical dreams of gold through the Orinoco delta, that Harriot changed his primary allegiance from Ralegh's household to that of the 9th Earl"; though he continued to serve both men faithfully for the rest of his life. While the prospect of a more secure and comfortable life style as a "gentleman pensioner", enabling him to devote most of his time to his intellectual interests, may have been in Harriot's mind for some time, it is suggested that the "trigger" was Ralegh's treatment of Sanderson. It is on that basis, too, that it is suggested[18] that Sanderson's detailed description of how the endorsement on the absolute release was forged, sixteen years later, in the 1611 litigation, was derived from inside information supplied by Harriot. This ties in with Harriot's evidence in the litigation, generally agreed to be "unsatisfactory", when he had the impossible task of (i) avoiding incriminating his employer, Ralegh (ii) avoiding incriminating himself and (iii) telling the truth on oath. So, while denying that he had tampered with the document, he admitted that it was possible that the release had been "modified" by someone else without his involvement. Answers to interrogatories are normally prepared by a lawyer and it is not difficult to imagine John Shelbury carefully preparing the uninformative and unsatisfactory drafts for Harriot's signature.

A few hours after the dramatic scene at Plympton, probably on 6th. February 1595, Ralegh set sail out of Plymouth for South America. Around the 5th September in the same year Ralegh was back in Plymouth. The expedition had been eventful but could hardly be regarded as a success, though Ralegh brought back some rock samples, some found to contain gold, and some pearls and precious stones.[19] Early in 1596 Ralegh published his "Discoverie of the Large, Rich and Beautiful Empyre of Guiana" which, in a manner reminiscent of the "Brief and True Report of the new found land of Virgina", lauded the potential of the country and Ralegh's enlightened attitude to the native population, making a case for Guyana to be developed as a Ralegh "sphere of influence" in order to shut out the normal, rapacious Englishmen. "The book sold widely, and was a greater success than the voyage"[20] Ralegh's book "toned down" a number of incident where his men had employed force and entirely omitted the disastrous arrack on Cumana.[21]

While the 1595 expedition was a failure, Ralegh's promotion of Guyana as a repository of gold and other riches reached the public consciousness and was featured by Shakespeare in the Merry Wives of Windsor, written in 1597. Sir John Falstaff is wooing Mistress Ford and Mistress Page, fancies that they are both attracted to him and prepares love letters to them. Regarding Mistress Page, he says "Here's another letter to her: she bears the purse too;[22] she is a region in Guiana, all gold and bounty. I will be 'cheator[23] to them both and they shall be exchequers to me; they shall be my East and West Indies, and I will trade to them both. Go bear thou this letter to Mistress Page; and thou this to Mistress Ford. We will thrive, lads, we will thrive".[24] In view of Falstaff's obviously unprincipled intentions towards the married women, perhaps Shakespeare is targeting Ralegh and other international "exploiters" as well as introducing a topical allusion.

No doubt news of the quarrel between the two men spread but this did not adversely affect Sanderson's public standing: indeed, in view of Ralegh' unpopularity, it might well have enhanced it. The only letter from Sanderson to Lord Salisbury which survives is endorsed 16th September 1595 and, by its context, is connected with Raleigh's return from the search for El Dorado.[25] This letter is important both for its contents and for its broader implications. As to the contents, first, Sanderson returns to Cecil some of the "ore", having had the balance "refined". This looks like part of the mineral specimens just brought back by Ralegh from Guyana, which Cecil, who had invested personally in the voyage, as Sanderson would have been well aware, has distributed for analysis: sadly, Sanderson does not report the results of his tests. Secondly, he sends a "sea card" of the West Indies, possibly a local chart, a "little terrestrial globe, obviously one of the small Molyneux globes, with "the latin book that teaches the use of my great globes, probably Hues' work "Tractatus de Globis", which, ironically, was dedicated to Ralegh, with a table at the end "of places marked thereon and upon many sea cards", and a Spanish book that he may read about the province of Guyana, but wishes the book returned. The bearer of Sanderson's letter appears to be his nephew John Janes, who sailed with John Davis in his first and third NW Passage voyages as Sanderson's representative. Janes obviously became attached to Davis and accompanied him when he joined Cavendish's disastrous second voyage 1591–3, so that in the letter to Salisbury Sanderson reports that (Janes) "my kinsman hath been as near the poles of the world as any man in England. He tells me he hath seen above 20 men at one time together with heads like dogs." This is a reference to one of the many travellers' tales reported by Raleigh, which were ridiculed on his return, though some corroboration came in later from Spanish sources. Sanderson quotes Janes, who wrote an account of the voyage, as providing additional corroboration. It is interesting that Janes, who wrote the account of this voyage by Davis, describes dog-faced men encountered in the Magellan Strait, "There came a great multitude of Salvages to the ship, throwing dust in the ayre, leaping and running like brute beasts, having vizards (i.e. masks) on their faces like dogs faces, or else their faces are dogs faces indeed". This story may be connected with similar reports from Patagonia of giant men with heads like dogs. Such creatures are shown on the Piri Reis world map of 1513, together with four other clearly delineated animals native to South America: these four other species still survive in the areas where they are shown on the map; while the dog-headed giants have been provisionally identified as a form of giant sloth (mylodon) now extinct.

Switching now to the wider implications of the letter, we may note the following (i) Sanderson is clearly on familiar terms with Salisbury, sending presents, lending a book and so on, as well as responding to the business in hand – the analysis of the mineral ore (ii) In sending the letter, presents &c. by the hand of his nephew John Janes, and mentioning his seagoing experience, he may be seeking to persuade Salisbury to "notice" Janes (iii) By quoting Janes' experience with the dog-headed men, he is effectively combatting the ridicule being cast on his uncle-in-law, despite their angry breach seven months before (iv) Salisbury's reliance on Sanderson to arrange analysis of the ore confirms that he is recognised as having some expertise in minerals (v) the relaxed relationship with Salisbury, and Salisbury's reliance on Sanderson over the ore, corroborates the statements made as to his intimacy with senior statesmen by Sir William in An Answer.

12

The Curious Incident of the Dog
In the Night-Time

Following the quarrel with Ralegh in January – February 1595 Sanderson never, so far as is known, worked with him again; though he seems still to have been engaged, on Ralegh's behalf, in the realisation of the Madre de Dios treasure in 1602.[1] Harriot became his finance manager and John Shelbury replaced Sanderson as Ralegh's representative with regard to the wine import and retailing licences[2] and the export of undyed broadcloths.

With Ralegh safely home, Sanderson might, according to Raleigh's "imposed" conditions, be called upon at any time to justify his accounts all over again – covering cash transactions for some eight or more years down to 1595, and after having had his receipts, vouchers, cancelled bonds, paperwork &c. confiscated. But nothing happened – until sixteen years later. If nothing else, the "failure of the dog to bark"[3] after Ralegh's safe return, suggests that (i) the Ralegh team did not really think that Sanderson had short-changed them (ii) they had no intention of asking the Chancery Court to order complete re-accounting unless and until Sanderson showed signs of demanding reimbursement of what he was owed and threatening or commencing proceedings. (iii) the claim for re-accounting was therefore not a bona fide claim but an artificial device to be used only as a pre-emptive strike weapon.

Both men went on with their respective lives, and, remarkably, despite the unpleasant scene which had terminated their close commercial collaboration, some form of cordial social intercourse continued between the Raleghs and the Sandersons. We can only guess that, on cool reflection, Sanderson decided that he must separate business and social considerations, deal with the financial loss as best he could and continue to be friendly and respectful towards a Ralegh whose reputation was again on the rise.

Alternatively, we may conclude that Sanderson, despite the provocation, was unable to throw off the awe, the hero-worship, the engrained respect, which he had nurtured for his younger uncle-in-law over the previous eleven years. It is possible that the two wives had something to do with maintaining the social relationship. After all, the Sandersons had entertained Bess and her husband in London and Essex, when they were newly (and hastily) married and had been banished from Court in disgrace; and Margaret Sanderson may well have insisted that the Sandersons should remain on friendly terms with her uncle's family.

There is no definite record of the two men meeting until the encounter on Hounslow Heath in 1603, but the conversation reported on that occasion (and the tears) suggest that social contact had continued, acknowledgment of the debts had been given and relations were friendly and not simply a matter of public show.

However, before picking up on the ongoing activities of the two principals, we must construct a framework, or at least a working hypothesis, to explain how Sanderson was driven in 1613 to borrow from a notorious moneylender, one George Pitt, the comparatively tiny sum of £100. (The £100 quickly increased, partly by Pitt's trickery and partly because Sanderson had to pay additional claims which came in later, to around £550; and when Sanderson failed to repay he was committed to debtors' prisons, where he stayed for about eight years until 1622: this is discussed more fully, below at p. 116ff.)

Coming back to February 1595, Sanderson owed around £1,700, probably to a City friend or contact. Based on the expected duration of the Manoa/El Dorada expedition the loan was likely to be for 1–2 years. With such a loan some extension of time could usually be negotiated, but a monetary penalty would be payable, over and above the interest which would run on (probably at or around 10% p.a). On this occasion an extension might have been more difficult to arrange since the expedition was over in a few months – and it had been patently unsuccessful, despite the puffing account which Ralegh hurried to publish. Against this, Sanderson's personal credit was high – it was not long since (in 1590) he had borrowed £5,000 from John Watts without security to prop up the efforts to relieve the Roanoke settlement.

We do not know for certain what Sanderson chose to do. He must have realised that, on the one hand, he must get rid of this expensive short term loan as quickly as possible, but that, on the other hand, as soon as it was known that he had done so any chance of Ralegh reimbursing him would become extremely remote. We have already made the assumption that Sanderson had accepted that Ralegh was not going to reimburse him at once, perhaps never, and had decided, for a range of reasons, not to press him for payment. Despite his evident affection and respect for Ralegh over the 10–11 years to 1595 Sanderson must have realised that Ralegh's protestations and promises to pay were worth little. It is therefore suggested that Sanderson probably settled with his lender after about three years, say in 1598, and that it cost him about £4,000 when interest and penalties had been added to the sum originally outstanding.

Where did Sanderson find the cash to repay his lender? Here, too, there is no information. If the rent-roll from the Sanderson family property portfolio was £700 p.a. the value of the portfolio might have been some £15,000 but it is never easy to turn property into cash under pressure, and one cannot see the Sanderson family welcoming a sell-off of inherited assets to relieve what they may well have regarded as an imprudent entanglement taken on by the head of the family.[4] Sanderson's import-export activities would be generating some excess of cash. Further, there was the cash from the rent-roll itself. So it is reasonable to assume that he was able to find the money, accept the serious reduction in his net worth and perhaps "draw in his horns" temporarily.

We still need to explain the transition from Sanderson's "business as usual" position in 1598, or whenever he actually paid off his own lender, to the "cash crisis" around 1613 and the resort to the moneylender. In 1603 there was the renewed expression of regret and the promise to pay, accompanied by tears, on Hounslow Heath, though by then Ralegh had lost most of his royal perquisites and was about to be convicted for treason and attainted – thus being deprived of his assets; so that his promises were even more hollow and less credible than before. Most writers suggest that Sanderson must have suffered a second financial blow, sufficient to render him insolvent and to push him, at last, into making a formal demand on Ralegh for reimbursement. By then Ralegh's personal property had been vested in two administrators, Shelbury (his solicitor) and one Robert Smith, who were authorised by Salisbury to pay his debts and support his wife and son; so that the formal demand went to them, not to Ralegh personally[5] Sanderson tells us[6] that the administrators launched the Chancery action requiring re-accounting in 1611 "under instructions from Ralegh"[7] because he had made the formal demand for reimbursement. This demand was probably made only a few weeks earlier, since the Ralegh camp had long had the pre-emptive strike weapon ready for use.

What was this second financial blow? Previous writers have suggested as the cause either unsuccessful property speculation or excessive litigation:[8] but there is no evidence supporting this. In assessing the evidentiary value of An Answer we noticed[9] that Sir William's narrative becomes laconic, less fluent and sometimes obscure when he refers to his father's financial problems: he is clearly embarrassed. Thus, in dealing with the allegation made in "Observations" that his father was thrown into prison on account of debts owing to Ralegh. Sir William in An Answer roundly denies this. He does not, however, go on to state that his father was indeed thrown into a debtors' prison *but that this was done by another creditor* – clearly, for this to happen, his ready money must have been exhausted and his credit destroyed. When, therefore, Sir William states quite explicitly that Sanderson became involved in farming the Mines Royal *"to his great cost and losse"*, we must sit up and take notice; and it is hardly necessary to go looking for other causes.[10] Substantial investment in mining; taking on mining leases, which seems to have been the way in which Mines Royal operations were "farmed"; providing working capital and giving guarantees to support third parties who got involved, would be quite sufficient to produce a major liquidity crisis when the farmed mining operations realised losses and the cash flow turned negative. It seems likely that Sanderson's past experience as a merchant buying and selling goods and employing merchant ships on trading, privateering or exploration voyages proved insufficient to prepare him for the quite different problems of managing in an extractive industry, in which the products might prove to be unsuitable for their intended purpose or too expensive, or indeed both. There are several recorded examples of farmers of the Mines Royal and the Minerals and Battery companies' activities sustaining major losses, for example, Sanderson's fellow-economist Gerald Malynes.

If mining losses produced the second financial blow (which seem to be the inescapable conclusion), what happened next? When losses occur in any enterprise and cash starts to haemorrhage there is a range of remedial steps which can be taken.[11] The first choice is whether to keep the business running in hope that losses may be reversed, or to stop trading and pay off the parties involved. In many cases, if the first is attempted and fails, it is followed by the second; and additional cash will be needed. The investor will need to turn assets into cash, call in outstanding debts and perhaps borrow. Once difficulties are apparent, however, the situation changes dramatically: credit dries up, debts become difficult to collect, lenders on reasonable terms cannot be found. We do not know exactly what occurred, but it looks as though the formal demand on Ralegh's administrators in 1611 was part of a painful exercise of this kind, accompanied by the sudden disappearance of Sanderson's "undoubted credit" in the City of London.

The key pointer in this hypothesis is the fact that in 1613 .Sanderson borrowed initially from George Pitt only the tiny sum of £100. That he had to go to a moneylender at all demonstrates that his credit standing in the City, once "undoubted", had disappeared. That he needed to borrow only £100 initially suggests that he was very nearly successful in closing down his mining investment and settling all claims. We know that the second loan of £450 from Pitt was taken so that Sanderson could pay off some claims on guarantees which he had given – which came in later than the main claims.[12]

This working hypothesis explaining the collapse of Sanderson's fortunes in the 1603–1613 period will provide a background for the ongoing narrative as we return to 1595.

Ralegh was creeping back into favour with the Queen. He sent out two further expeditions to Guyana by the end of 1596. He personally distinguished himself in the 1596 Cadiz Expedition, collecting booty of some £1,800, and again in the following year in the Islands Voyage to the Azores. He organised privateering expeditions; acquired the freehold reversion to the Sherborne Estate and settled it on Wat, and started exploiting his Irish estates by granting leases and then (in 1602–3) selling out altogether for £1,500 to Robert Boyle, who became the first Earl of Cork. By 1602 the new Sherborne Lodge and the park had been completed to Ralegh's satisfaction. Ralegh had discovered that John Meere, his disastrous choice as steward at Sherborne, had been forging his (Ralegh's) signature and tried to dismiss him in 1602, but Meere sued in Star Chamber and seems to have hung on at the Castle, conducting a guerrilla war against his "employer".

During the same eight year period (1595–1603) less is known of Sanderson's activities. Certainly, as already noted, he continued to promote the Molyneux globes, and he supported John Norden's Speculum Britanniae (English county guides, providing maps and descriptions).[13] In 1598 the Court of the Fishmongers' Company noted that Sanderson owed £10, being his share in a loan raised by the Queen from the City of London and apportioned by the Lord Mayor to the various livery companies.[14] It is tempting to guess that this is a straw in the wind, indicating the onset of Sanderson's cash problems, but this seems unlikely since the amount is very small and there were some 85 other defaulters (for similar amounts) among the Fishmongers, who were one of the richest of the livery companies. There is a similar unpaid contribution dating from 1609 (for £8, and, here too, there are other fishmongers who had failed to pay) but this fell into the time of Sanderson's financial problems and it may well be that he by then had reason to ignore this modest amount.[15]

We will now divert to describe his involvement with John Norden.

John Norden's Speculum Britanniae

Sanderson's patronage of John Norden, the famous English map-maker, came to light only recently, perhaps in 1935, when the arms on a

Hampshire map derived from a Norden MS map were identified as being those of Sanderson, in the "enhanced" form directed by Queen Elizabeth.[16] While it was customary for map publishers to dedicate their products to the monarch or to a local magnate, or to embellish their maps with the heraldic arms of local dignitaries, to find the arms of a City merchant, with no other connections with the localities in question, displayed in this way, suggests that he was the financial supporter of the publishing enterprise; though, as yet, there seems to be no further evidence to support this. Sanderson may have been introduced to John Norden either by Lord Burghley, who supported him, or by William Camden, who included maps by Norden in his "Britannia"

John Norden was born c.1548, attended Hart Hall Oxford, from the 1580s and wrote devotional books but by the end of the decade he was practising as a land lawyer which led him into surveying. In the 1590s., with support from Lord Burghley, he commenced surveying in preparation for a series of English county guide books, under the title "Speculum Britanniae". Maps and text were produced around 1595 and the original MS maps of Hampshire and Sussex, amongst others, survive.[17] The project seems to have faltered around 1598 either on account of of the death of Lord Burghley or because Norden was associated with the Earl of Essex, but around 1600 some of the MS maps were engraved as county maps and published; the maps of Hampshire and Sussex bearing Sanderson's arms. None of these appears to have survived but the maps were copied and published later (by Peter Stent/John Overton c.1642–80) and a few copies survive from this "second edition".[18] We do not know the exact nature of Sanderson's support but as only two counties bear his arms it looks as though either the project itself or Sanderson's support ran out of steam. By 1605 Norden seems to have abandoned the Speculum Britanniae when he was appointed surveyor to the Duchy of Cornwall; and for the rest of his life (he died in 1626) he practised as an estate surveyor; producing among other books, "The Surveyor's dialogue" in 1607, a manual for surveyors, which ran into many editions.

In 1603 Queen Elizabeth died, James I succeeded and by 20th July Raleigh was in the Tower. Cecil's briefings against Raleigh, followed by his own discourteous conduct to the King at their first meeting, led to his being stripped of his Royal gifts, appointments and perquisites and prosecuted for treason. We have earlier[19] described the meeting between Ralegh and Sanderson on Hounslow Heath in November 1603.

Ralegh's conviction was followed by the cruel pantomime of last minute reprieve on the scaffold and indefinite imprisonment in the Tower. As the nightmare of immediate execution faded he settled to a reasonably comfortable and sociable existence, with his fellow prisoner

Northumberland, who joined him in the Tower following the Gunpowder Plot in 1605, and to a limited degree with Lord Cobham, concentrating on intellectual and scientific activities and writing a number of books. He was permitted visits by his coterie of Harriot, Hues, Shelbury, Keymis and others, and was soon joined by Bess.[20] Sir William in An Answer suggests that, at this stage too, his father had a hand in helping the Raleghs, "For after Sir Walter's Sentence; and Reprieve to the Tower close prisoner, (and friendless, he saies) only Mr Lassells,[21] my Ladies friend, did not leave her. This Gentleman can tell, that Mr Sanderson, by his interest with the Lord Treasurer Salisbury, procured the effect and prayer of her Petition, to visit her husband, and to be close prisoner with him; and but time, for it is said, she suddainly conceived".[22] Carew Ralegh was baptised on 15th February 1605 in the chapel of St. Peter ad Vincula within the Tower. It seems that, once Ralegh had been removed to the Tower, and his propensity for trouble-making cut off, Salisbury may have been influenced by the surge of popularity which had followed his brave defiance at his trial, and maybe even from some sense of guilt, and did what he could to make his life tolerable. When trouble started on the Sherborne estate, with John Meere prominent – rents were withheld and timber was felled – Salisbury arranged (in 1604) for the appointment of two of Ralegh's loyal servants or retainers, John Shelbury (his solicitor) and Robert Smith as trustees or administrators of such of his property as had not already been forfeited, to pay Ralegh's debts and maintain Bess and young Wat.[23] In this way the effect of attainder was modified or at least delayed, though the exact legal basis is not clear. For example, in January 1609, Ralegh directed the administrators to assign a lease without consideration to John Meere . It has, incidentally, been suggested that the letter of instructions was another of Meere's forgeries.[24] The effect of this transaction was to reduce the value of the property destined for the Crown. Again, the administrators carried out exchanges of property with the King; and in 1611 they commenced the proceedings against Sanderson, apparently without any official permission or authority, but on Raleigh's directions. Since these proceedings seem to have had little chance of success[25] such a step would be more likely to reduce rather than to increase the value of the Crown's expectations.under the attainder. In short, it looks as though, under the general cover of the legal concept of "attainder" Salisbury was left with discretion to do what he thought best.

In 1605 a flaw was discovered in Ralegh's settlement of Sherborne on Wat, so that the entire freehold was forfeit to the Crown, not just Ralegh's life interest. This devastating blow was, to a degree, mitigated by the grant by the Crown (in 1609) of £8000 compensation to Bess plus an annuity of £400 to her and Wat during their lives.[26] In the same year Ralegh gained the friendship of Queen Anne after prescribing her his secret "cordial", which she believed had restored her health, and through her he was introduced to Prince Henry.[27] The Queen, Prince Henry and the Queen's brother, King Christian of Denmark, who visited England in 1606, all pleaded with James I, in the event without success, for Ralegh's release, though Ralegh paid the Prince much attention and gained his admiration and affection. Ralegh hoped, too, with some justification, that the Prince would bring about the restoration of Sherborne. He also dedicated to the Prince his History of the World, started around 1607. Prince Henry was a serious, charming and exceptionally intelligent young man, with wide interests including sports (except hunting – his father's passion), politics, foreign affairs, shipping, military matters and overseas colonisation – all matters in which Raleigh could demonstrate his mastery. There were others seeking the patronage of the young Prince as well. In 1604 the Lord High Admiral had a scaled-down ship built for him by the shipwright Phineas Pett, named "Disdain"; books were dedicated to him: in 1607 Pett planned another ship, a three-decker to be named "Prince Royal", presenting a model to the Prince, and in 1608 her keel was laid; and in 1612 the expedition sent out by a City syndicate to seek the NW Passage under Sir Thomas Button enjoyed his patronage. Sanderson, too, sought and obtained the Prince's friendship, as we have described earlier[28], perhaps seeking to align his efforts alongside those of Ralegh, who looked to the Prince to help him regain his freedom and recover Sherborne. The Prince is said to have declared, "No one but my father would keep such a bird in a cage"[29]

Sadly, Prince Henry died in 1612, probably from typhoid, and Raleigh's plans for freedom and Sherborne perished with him.

Following his conviction and reprieve in 1603 Ralegh remained some 13 years in the Tower. We noted above Sanderson's efforts with Salisbury to get permission for Bess to join her husband in the Tower. Further, Sir William confirms that the relationship between the families continued., "….Sir Walter Raleigh, with whom, in the Tower, my Father and Mother, my selfe and brethren, were very often, in visits of civility, and respect to each other; and afterwards, even at his Chamber dore, the night before he suffered". Sanderson was himself in prison, albeit as a debtor, from around 1613 until 1622 so no doubt he had to obtain leave from his gaoler to take his family to visit his uncle-in-law during this period. Following Prince Henry's death in 1612 Ralegh switched his hopes of release to a further expedition to Guyana. His North American patent had been forfeited in 1603: others had taken up the work and Jamestown was founded in 1607.

We now divert to describe Sanderson's disastrous involvement in mining.

13

A Mining Disaster

We have noted two or three sightings of Sanderson and his family helping the Raleghs or showing respect to Ralegh himself in the years after 1603, but, apart from this, the little information which we have points to his investment in a new field, namely mining: Sir William explains in An Answer: "And being very well seen in the matter of Monies and Oar, he farmed of King James the Mines Royal of England, and so set hundreds of men at work, to his great expense and losse, in Darbyshire, Worcestershire, Devon &c. whereabouts I have been often with him." Virtually no other evidence of this activity has yet come to light. The Mines Royal Company and its sister company, the Mineral and Battery Works Company received their original charters of incorporation as joint stock companies in 1568. They were formed as part of a plan, probably conceived and certainly promoted by Lord Burghley, to encourage mining and metalworking in England by importing specialist skill from Germany and Austria, which at that time predominated in mining, the treatment of ores and in metalworking, particularly the manufacture of ordnance. The usual Tudor method of stimulating activity without the need for Government funding was employed – the companies were granted monopolies: the Mines Royal Company had the monopoly of mining in Wales and the counties of York, Cumberland, Westmorland, Cornwall, Devon, Gloucester and Worcester, while the Mineral and Battery Works Company was allotted the rest of England and the Pale of Ireland in respect of mining and, apart from that, carried out metal working. It is not clear why two separate companies were needed and there were in fact overlaps, for example, the Mines Royal Company did undertake some metal working activities. The members and assistants (i.e. directors) of the companies were drawn from the nobility, landowners and City men – Sir Thomas Smythe[1] was prominent and one or two outstanding Germans,

- 95 -

The Mines Royal Company

The Minerals and Battery Works Company

particularly Daniel Houghsetter and Christopher Schutz. The policies, or the practices, of the two companies differed, in that the key German specialists retained the management of the Mines Royal, while in the sister company the German experts introduced their know-how and trained up the Englishmen. There is no doubt that Burghley's initiative succeeded in developing this industry in England, but the history is extremely complicated, with many mines being worked all over England and Wales. The position was further confused by traditional claims to mineral rights being made by large landowners and by the prerogative right claimed by the Crown to a monopoly for the mining of gold; and there were many legal disputes. There were also some social problems with the introduction of German "guest-workers" into remote rural locations. In earlier days, the companies themselves worked the mines but from around 1600 when profitability was poor the companies granted leases to third parties. It looks as though this was the way in which Sanderson became involved. There seems no reason to doubt the accuracy of Sir William's account in An Answer, particularly as he refers to the large losses which his father incurred.[2] The scale of involvement must have been substantial: Sir William refers to "Darbyshire, Worcester, Devon &c" and states that he has often accompanied his father on visits. – he was by then in his early 20s. Beyond this we have a few references to Sanderson being involved in activities related to mining, set out below.

Full records of the proceedings of the Courts of both companies, the Mines Royal and the Minerals and Battery, have survived, in one MS version,[3] but unfortunately a number of pages covering the years in which Sanderson might have been involved are missing. However, from a different source we learn that he was around 1600 a member of the Minerals and Battery Compny and as such involved in at least two Star Chamber suits started by John Brode over the Isleworth Copper Mill i.e. not about mining as such and not concerning the Mines Royal Company.[4]

Sir William mentioned Sanderson's involvement in "Derbyshire, Worcester and Devon &c.". Derbyshire fell in the Minerals and Battery Works territory, while the other two named counties were under the Mines Royal; so "farming the Mines Royal" seems not quite an accurate description of Sanderson's activities. It seems likely that Sir William, writing over 50 years later, produced a garbled account – but there is no doubt about the "large losse" which Sir William recorded.

We have noted Sanderson's involvement on behalf of Lord Bughley in tests carried out on ore brought back from South America by Ralegh in 1592.

There survive some fragmentary court records of a dispute between Sanderson and Sir John Zouche of Codnor in Derbyshire, dating from

1609. Sir John "was typical of many Elizabethan gentlemen, in that he was high-spirited, ambitious and short of money".[5] He was a large landowner who made many efforts to exploit minerals and get involved in metal working: in general he was not very successful: "any scheme in which Sir John Zouche was involved, however, was most likely to fail".[6] It appears that Sanderson lent Sir John £500 which was not repaid; he obtained judgment against him in 1602 and when this was not obeyed he obtained a Court order for Sir John to divert to him part of the rents of his estate, but he defaulted, so Sanderson had to go back to court. The eventual outcome is unknown. While this does not look like "farming the Mines Royal" it does have some connection with mining and metalwork, thus providing some limited corroboration of Sir William's story. It may be, too, that Sanderson never recovered the £500 (perhaps £60,000 to-day) in which case that sum would swell the "mining losses" which he evidently suffered.

14

In Chancery and Star Camber

In 1611 Ralegh's administrators, on Ralegh's instructions, commenced proceedings in the Chancery Court against Sanderson, seeking an order that his treasury transactions down to 1595 should be re-accounted for. This was in response to Sanderson's formal demand for the payment of the money owed to him by Ralegh, out of the funds which the administrators had been authorised by Salisbury to collect to pay his debts and support Bess and Wat Ralegh.. The originating document, the bill of complaint, has not survived, but there are a large number of other documents, many in a poor and scarcely legible condition. The general lines of the case, and of the subsequent proceedings which Sanderson commenced against Ralegh and his team in Star Chamber, have been well described by Dr. Shirley[1] at a time when no doubt the documents were in better condition.[2] While the overall picture is fairly clear, there are a number of problems resulting from the practice under which court records were preserved:- (i) what we have are the formal written documents exchanged between the parties and witnesses – originating documents, defence and counterclaim, replication, interrogatories and their answers, and so on (ii) there are no records of what was said or what happened in the court hearings, though there are a few references in the later documents as to what happened in earlier hearings (iii) there is no record of the outcome – judgment(s), settlement, abandonment of proceedings. In particular, it is important to treat carefully any apparent "statements of fact" in these documents. Some occur in "pleadings" i.e. the Court documents, making or rebutting the legal claims, and some in interrogatories, statements made by witnesses under oath. The former are not "evidence" at all and the latter have not been tested in Court by cross-examination, so are likely to be "unreliable" even though "made under oath".[3] One or two blatant examples are noted where they occur, for example, John Meere's views on the use of the place name "Gwyana" to describe part of South America.

The Chancery Proceedings

Ralegh, through his administrators, John Shelbury (his solicitor) and Robert Smith, sought re-examination of the accounts on which Ralegh had granted Sanderson a release in 1595. Although Sanderson in his petition to Star Chamber in 1613 said that it had been alleged that he had dealt fraudulently with Raleigh, it seems that the plaint claimed only that the accounts were "uncertain", "not true" and were "general", that is, not sufficient detailed i.e. fraud was not alleged. It was suggested, too, by the Ralegh camp that Sanderson had not properly accounted for £60,000. This is, by any standards, an enormous sum, in present-day terms some £8 million, and, even more startling, is about half the total amount of money which passed through the hands of Ralegh and/or Sanderson, as his treasurer, in the ten years prior to 1595.[4] It is also considerably more than the cost of the El Dorado expedition in 1595 on its own (thought to be around £40,000) thus confirming that the re-accounting claim was not confined to the Manao/El Dorado expedition but went back a number of years.

Sanderson put in an "Answer". First, he acknowledged the appointment of the administrators to pay Ralegh's debts and maintain Bess and Wat. He admits that he cannot now remember all the disbursements "for that it is about 17 years ago since...the passing of his account". He maintained that his accounts were honest and accurate "for anything [he] knows or remembers or for any objection or exception that as yet was or could be taken thereunto by any honest understanding man in accounts that [he] had heard of". Then he launched into the story[5] of accompanying Ralegh to Plymstock, the negotiation and delivery of the release to himself and his release to Ralegh, and then the trick by which Ralegh recovered possession of the release which he had given to Sanderson, and, finally, Ralegh's attempt to impose retrospectively the conditions about whether he died or not on the voyage, by handing the release to Thomas Harriot. He described his anger and his upbraiding of Raleigh's behaviour after accepting many years of unpaid efforts, at a time when Sanderson has borrowed, on his own credit, and made over to Ralegh some £1,600 or £1,700. He then switches to a legal argument, saying that Ralegh's handing over the release to Harriot, purportedly "in escrow"[6] was ineffective, since the release in absolute, unqualified terms, had previously been formally "signed, sealed and delivered" by Ralegh and handed to Sanderson some days earlier. He added that he had tried in every way, though without success, to get the release from Harriot in whose possession he had recently seen it. He asks for the plaint to be dismissed with costs.

In addition, Sanderson entered a "counter-suit" or counterclaim for the monies owed to him by Ralegh.

The administrators, Shelbury and Smith, submitted a "replication". They described the meticulous cash books kept by Sanderson, one for receipts and one for disbursements (they appear to have been somewhat surprised at how thorough he was) and suggested that production of them would satisfy the plaintiffs' claims. They maintained that Sanderson's claim that Ralegh owed him on the accounts some £300 was ridiculous since "when he first dealt for Sir Walter Raleigh was hardly worth the sum he demandeth...but lived and maintained himself, his wife and family" at Ralegh's charge. Apart from being irrelevant, this is another example of obvious falsehood, concerning facts of which the two administrators had no knowledge. Further, they said "that the said account which Sanderson delivered[7] is absurd and uncertain and no man is able to find out the truth thereof" In view of the audit carried out for Ralegh by Harriot this is strong stuff. Finally, they rubbished Sanderson's statement that Ralegh had asked him to assist with "the better furnishing and setting forth to the sea" of the ships engaged in the 1595 Manao/El Dorado voyage on the basis he had nothing to teach Ralegh about ship management. In view of Sanderson's experience this statement, too, is worthless.

Evaluating the Claim made on Ralegh's behalf

To summarise:-

Ralegh. Please order Sanderson to re-account for all transactions down to 1595.

Sanderson. This was done in 1595 and audited by Harriot, and Ralegh gave me a formal, unconditional, release

Ralegh The release was not absolute: if I came home safely Sanderson had to re-account for all transactions

(1) First, the possibility of fraud may be discussed and discarded. If Sanderson had deliberately falsified his accounts and in this way obtained a release, the Chancery Court would re-open and re-examine the accounts *after any lapse of time – but only if the complainant came to Court promptly after discovering the fraud*. Waiting 16 years is not "promptly", but, in any case, there does not seem to be any allegation of fraud in the surviving documents.

(2) If Ralegh's formal release was absolute i.e. not subject to any conditions, in the absence of fraud (see above) *the Court would refuse to re-open settled accounts*.

(3) If Ralegh's formal release is construed by the Court as being conditional i.e the parties have agreed that if Ralegh comes home safely Sanderson must re-justify all transaction down to 1595, the Court is likely to reject the claim made on Ralegh's behalf for re-accounting on either of two grounds (i) because of 16 years unexplained delay since Ralegh got home (ii) because of "acquiescence" i.e. the Court would interpret 16 years unexplained delay as abandonment by the complainant of any claim which he might once have had.

(4) The likelihood of rejection under (3) (i) would be increased as soon as it appeared that Sanderson no longer had the evidence to justify many years of cash transactions in the distant past; and the likelihood of rejection would be *further* increased as soon as it appeared that the complainant had deliberately deprived Sanderson of such evidence.

These conclusions are based on the principles or rules of "equity".[8] These were the principles applied in the Chancery Courts. Unlike the rules of "law" applied in the other Courts, which were fixed and consant, the equitable principles took account of the actual circumstances in every case and the actual conduct of the parties, so as to arrive at a just and equitable decision. This objective is sometimes expressed by saying that "the Chancery Court is a court of conscience".[9]

It is thus clear that, on the pleadings, the case advanced for Ralegh was extremely weak and likely to fail. It seems that this was not lost on the judge, Sir Edward Phelips, the Master of the Rolls: he was an experienced and highly successful lawyer, who had practised in Chancery and Star Chamber, and at the same time followed a political career. He was MP for Bere Alston, Weymouth, Penrhyn and Andover and junior knight of the shire for Somerset, and in 1604 was elected Speaker of the House of Commons. In January 1611, at around the age of 56, he was appointed Master of the Rolls, so this was one of his early cases as a judge.[10] Phelips was always a government man and it is therefore reasonable to expect that he would not be prejudiced in favour of Ralegh; would not be overly impressed by Ralegh's private letter to him after he had started hearing the case, dealt with below, and, if the case, as pleaded, looked weak would react accordingly.[11] If the Master of the Rolls seemed to be tending against Ralegh this would have caused dismay, if not panic, in the Ralegh camp. Their morale must have been further depressed by the realisation that the plan based on a pre-emptive strike had failed – by counterclaiming *in the same action* for the monies owed by Ralegh, Sanderson had avoided the need to go to another court to seek re-imbursement; which might have been prevented by order of the Chancery Court.

It appears that the case was heard on four or more separate days, with intervals in between. It was thus not until the third day's hearing, held in May 1611, that the controversial release granted by Ralegh to Sanderson, and then snatched back and handed to Harriot, was presented to the Court by Ralegh's team. Its terms were as Sanderson had described, except that there was an endorsement on the back of the document, apparently in Ralegh's handwriting, in the following terms:-

"Memorandum that it is agreed that the release to be sealed by the honourable Sir Walter Raleigh to Mr. William Saunderson be sealed absolutely and without condition delivered yet shall be left with Mr. Thomas Harriott to be by him kept until Sir Walter Raleigh returns from his intended voyage of Gwyana.

And that if the said Sir Walter Raleigh shall not return in the said voyage but die therein It is agreed that the said release shall be delivered to Mr. Saunderson for his discharge against Sir Walter Raleigh's executors for all actions and accounts

And that if the said Sir Walter Raleigh return from the said voyage then the said Mr Harriott shall deliver the said release to the said Sir Walter Raleigh and the said Mr. Saunderson then to discharge himself of all actions and demands of the said Sir Walter Raleigh by true account and in the mean season Mr. Saunderson may have the release to show to his creditors for their better satisfaction therein bringing the same again to Mr. Harriott

Walter Raleigh William Saunderson [11]
Witnessed by us underwritten Chr. Harris Jo. Meere"

Sanderson exploded "This a false forged and counterfeit note or writing for there never was any such agreement between us, neither is this my name or my handwriting that is subscribed to the same". He also noted that the endorsement was not dated – normal practice with any formal legal document. Sanderson also demanded that interrogatories (formal questions to be answered on oath) be put to the individuals named as witnesses in the endorsement or otherwise involved, to check out whether the endorsement was genuine.

We will offer some comments on this dramatic development before returning to describe how the trial proceeded.

Comments on the Endorsement

(1) The terms of the endorsement follow generally the "unilateral, retrospective condition" which Ralegh had purported to impose verbally at Plymstock 16 years before (in 1595), as recounted by Sanderson

(2 However, there are three important differences, obviously directed to "demolishing" the absolute nature of the release granted by Ralegh to Sanderson in 1595. We may again see the hand of the sharp lawyer who is not quite as clever as he thinks – the likely candidate is again John Shelbury, assisted by John Meere.

   (i) At Plymstock in 1595 Ralegh, after tricking Sanderson into handing back the release, simply announced verbally, without consultation, still less agreement, that it would be conditional rather than absolute, as its terms stated. Now, all is agreed, signed and witnessed.

   (ii) At Plymstock Ralegh imposed conditions verbally. Now we have a formal legal document.

   (iii) At Plymstock Ralegh's conditions were retrospective – the release had been given to Sanderson some days before. Now (see (3) below) the endorsement purports to come before the release – landing the draftsman in a dilemma from which there is probably no credible escape.

(3) Without actually being dated, which Sanderson, or perhaps his lawyers, spotted at once, the endorsement purports to pre-date the release: note the words "*to be sealed by* the honourable Sir Walter Raleigh".(italics added) The draftsman is faced with a dilemma. If the endorsement pre-dates the release, why use an "endorsement" at all? Why not draft the release itself to reflect the parties' intentions, inserting whatever conditions were agreed? If the endorsement was signed and witnessed after the release, the endorsement would be void and ineffective under the principle of "repugnancy". Given a signed, sealed and delivered document, any subsequent document which purports to vary it or retrospectively impose conditions, is said to be "repugnant" to the first document and is therefore void and ineffective. No doubt this is why the draftsman omitted any date, a normal part of any formal document, in his unsuccessful effort to escape the dilemma. Here, it is suggested, is the first piece of internal evidence suggesting that the endorsement was forged.

(4) The doctrine of "repugnancy" may also apply to the main operative words of the endorsement, "it is agreed that the release to be sealed by the honourable Sir Walter Raleigh to Mr. William Saunderson *be sealed absolutely and without condition delivered yet shall be left with Mr. Thomas Harriott....*" (Italics added) The internal inconsistency is obvious, as are the pitiful efforts being made by the draftsman to "square the circle". Here, it is suggested, is the second piece of internal evidence suggesting forgery

(5) For reasons which will appear shortly the case did not return to court until November 1611. On that day Sanderson drew the Court's attention to another suspicious point in the endorsement, the statement that the release "shall be left with Mr. Thomas Harriott to be by him kept until Sir Walter Raleigh returns *from his intended voyage of Gwyana"*. (Italics added) Sanderson pointed out that before Raleigh set out for South America the name Gwyana was not in use in England and was only introduced by Raleigh himself after his return in September 1595; suggesting, in short, that the draftsman had given himself away over a peripheral detail.

Certainly the planned expedition was referred to in advance as being to Manoa or El Dorado. Dr. Shirley dismisses Sanderson's point and prefers a contradiction made by John Meere, whose views and "evidence" on South American geography must surely be rejected as worthless; though he (Dr Shirley) goes on to admit that he has found no earlier use of Gwyana or Guyana.[13] This point has recently been investigated, at the suggestion of the present writer, by the National Maritime Museum and the British Library, investigating all the maps and charts available to them prior to 1595.[14] Their conclusions bear out Sanderson's contention that the word was not used in England until Ralegh personally introduced it on his return. Sanderson knew all about the planned expedition, was knowledgeable in navigation and geography, so it may fairly be suggested that he was too intelligent to submit this evidence to support his allegation of forgery to Star Chamber, which he did a little later, unless he was sure of his ground. It is interesting to note, too, that when Sanderson wrote to Lord Saisbury on 16th September 1595 i.e a few weeks after Ralegh's return, he enclosed (amongst other things) "a *Spanish* book that he may read about *the province of Guayana;* but wishes the book returned" (Italics added)

Some corroboration for the argument that Ralegh personally introduced the name "Guyana" or Gwyana" to England after his return in August/September 1595 is provided by Ralegh himself. He hurried to produce an account of the voyage and published it early in 1596 as "The Discoverie of Guyana". Apart from the factual content he followed a somewhat unusual "line" – the voyage had been one of enlightened discovery and colonisation; the native population was to be delivered by Ralegh without exploitation to the beneficent sovereignty of Queen Elizabeth; to avoid development by other Englishmen (who might be less scrupulous than Ralegh) it would become a reserved "sphere of influence" for Ralegh; and, accordingly, charts, sailing directions &c. should be tightly controlled out of the public domain.[15] The selection of a new, distinctive name for the territory, instead of "El Dorado" or "Manao" which had been used to promote the voyage, would make a good headline to support the spun story.

It is suggested that the use of "Gwyana" in the endorsement is a third piece of internal evidence suggesting forgery, in some ways stronger precisely because it occurs in a non-essential detail on which the draftsman's concentration may have relaxed.

(6) The nature of the "condition" for which Ralegh's team was fighting so hard – that audited figures should stand if the debtor dies within six months of the completion of the audit but be totally re-examined if he survives beyond six months– is, to say the least, somewhat bizarre. It hardly suggests a bona fide belief that there was something wrong about the accounting. It is suggested that this is a fourth piece of internal evidence suggesting that the claim was bogus and/or the document was forged.

(7) Sanderson alleged, in his petition to Star Chamber, that the forgery was hatched because the Master of the Rolls appeared to be tending against Ralegh. This seems very likely, given the extreme weakness of Ralegh's case as set out in the pleadings and the experience of the judge, albeit only recently appointed. If a decision to forge an endorsement was taken, the pressure resulting from the urgent need to turn the tide in Ralegh's favour seems to have forced the mastermind, almost certainly John Shelbury, into errors and inconsistencies. We have noted, above, four specific, suspicious points, and the whole endorsement – with the patently obvious, laboured efforts to demolish the absolute nature of the release which Ralegh had handed to Sanderson – would put any experienced equity draftsman on the alert. It is suggested, therefore, that there is sufficient internal evidence to support the possibility and even the likelihood of forgery, even before the direct evidence of forgery which Sanderson offered later.

(8) We do not know whether this was the first occasion on which Ralegh's team and/or Shelbury was accused of forgery or other irregular conduct[16] but it was not the last. We suggested that the trick played by Ralegh at Plymstock, to get back the release, was probably designed by Shelbury. John Meere was an unsavoury character, with some mental problems, and a known forger, who had been jailed for coin clipping: Ralegh had, most unwisely, rescued him from gaol to become his steward at Sherborne.[17] In 1602 Ralegh tried, unsuccessfully, to dispense with his services when he caught him (Meere) practising writing Ralegh's signature. There have been other documents suspected of being forgeries by John Meere of Ralegh's handwriting or signature.[18]

The recent biography of Bess Ralegh describes how, over time, she took over the direction of the Ralegh legal team, despite the legal rules and social conventions which kept women out of financial and legal business.[19] In January 1625 proceedings by Bess, represented by John Shelbury, against Peter van Lore, a well-known London jeweller and banker, with whom Ralegh had done much business, was finally dismissed. The decision was based on her claim being stale, so the judge did not have to rule on the allegations made by van Lore that Bess's legal team had forged a letter relating to events from many years before. The case was over a fine pearl necklace which Ralegh had pawned to the jeweller many yeas before for £1000 and Bess claimed that he had sold it to another party for more than double that amount.

From 1624 Bess was trying to persuade the King and Parliament to "restore" her son Carew i.e. wipe out the effect of Ralegh's attainder. This was called "restitution" and could be either "of blood" i.e. restoring personal legitimacy to Ralegh's son, or "of lands", so that the son could recover land which his father had at the time of his attainder. The former was eventually (in 1628) approved by Parliament, the latter not. The targets at which Bess was aiming were the Sherborne estate and the 42,000 Irish acres which Ralegh sold to Robert Boyle. In parallel Bess attempted to challenge Boyle directly on his title to the land, on the basis that Boyle had paid an insufficient price.[20] On the face of it, the price indeed seems very low for 42,000 acres, until one considers (i) Ralegh as an absentee landlord, after an initial effort, had not developed the land successfully – Boyle subsequently did much better (ii) Ralegh had sold off many leases of land, and also a lease of the seignory itself, for cash, so what he sold to Boyle was not the freehold i.e. total ownership, but the reversions which would give possession only when the leases terminated. In fact Boyle "bought out" the leases immediately, probably for an additional £2,500, although Boyle maintained that he had to pay £2,700. Shelbury acted for Bess but Meere, ironically, turned up on Boyle's side and a letter, apparently in Ralegh's handwriting, was produced from Ralegh to his son Carew enjoining him never to question Boyle's title in view of the kindnesses extended by Boyle to Ralegh in the course of his final expedition to Guyana in 1617. It looks as though John Meere had forged the letter for Boyle, and, on this occasion, Shelbury, on Bess's behalf, was trying to expose the forgery. In the event Boyle, after paying some judicious bribes, retained his estates.

When viewed together with the suspicious endorsement on Ralegh's release submitted to the Chancery Court in 1611, these two similar examples (there may well be others not yet discovered) establish what criminal lawyers call "system" – a likelihood of guilt rather than of innocence or coincidence.

Bess Ralegh carried out a similar deception, not in a court of law, and, therefore, perhaps independently, without the support of John Shelbury, after Ralegh's execution in 1618.[21] As an early part of her campaign to promote Ralegh's posthumous reputation and boost her own position, she distributed copies of a letter which Ralegh had written to her from prison; while bidding her an affectionate farewell, it set out the property which he intended to come to her. The only problem was that the letter had been written fifteen years earlier in 1603, immediately before Ralegh's scheduled execution, and had never been published at that time.

In these days it comes initially as a shock to find that forgery and bribery were quite common in the 16th century as was the practice of letting the judge know that an important personage favours one of the parties to the case which he is trying. Sometimes a party obviously "in the right" for example, with a good title to land. would give a bribe "to be on the safe side", a kind of insurance policy. As we will see, shortly, even one of the parties himself may approach the judge.

Interrogatories are ordered

Whether or not he had been tending against Ralegh already, the Master of the Rolls clearly thought that there was a case to answer in Sanderson's accusation of forgery and he ordered interrogatories[22] relating to the alleged forgery to be administered to the parties involved where they lived. .This was at the hearing in May 1611 and the Court then adjourned so that the interrogatories could be administered. Around 50 interrogatories and some nine individuals were involved .

Sanderson, however, was unlucky. According to Sanderson's allegation, set out later in his petition to Star Chamber, John Shelbury (Ralegh's solicitor) cut out the key questions contained in the interrogatories before they were put to the witnesses, so answers were not obtained to the vital questions, and the only "unattached" party, Sir Christopher Harris, died before he could answer the interrogatories. The other answers added nothing on the forgery itself, but the answers give by Thomas Harriot are significant, in view of his pivotal position. It will be recalled that he (i) had been part of Ralegh's household – effectively his "chief of staff" – for the 10–11 year period when Sanderson acted as treasurer and banker, and must have got to know him and become familiar with his method of working; and would have seen that, under Sanderson's management, the necessary cash was always forthcoming to pay for whatever their principal wanted to do (ii) had audited and approved the accounts of all Sanderson's transactions over that period (iii) had heard his employer decree at Plymstock that the validity of Sanderson's release should depend, not on the accuracy or otherwise of the accounts, but on whether Ralegh survived the expedition (iv) since the last evening at Plymstock had been given possession of Ralegh's release to Sanderson. Did he retain possession after the case had started? If so, no forged endorsement or other alteration could have been added without Harriot giving up possession of it – having some idea (if not complete knowledge) of what was going on.- and regaining custody, with an opportunity to see what, if anything had been done. If, as perhaps seems more likely, the key release document had, at the start of the litigation, been taken from Harriot's possession by John Shelbury as Ralegh's solicitor and admistrator, and as nominal plaintiff in the litigation, Harriot would not have known, but might have suspected, that the release was being tampered with. It is hardly surprising, therefore. that his answers to the interrogatories were weak, evasive and unhelpful to someone seeking to find out what, if anything, happened to the release document. In summary he said (i) he had had the release in his possession since Plymstock but could not be certain that he had had possession at all times (ii) While he had possession of the release he did not require anyone to alter or add to it (iii) the release seems to be the same now as when it was delivered to him "without any thinge done to yt by this deponent or by his knowledge consent request or procurement". Harriot's biographer, Dr Shirley, appears embarrassed that Harriot is obviously telling less than he knows – but his position was impossible. He had to protect and not incriminate his employer, he had no wish or motive to damage Sanderson, nor did he himself want to be a party to forgery. It is interesting to consider who drafted Harriot's replies to the interrogatories: almost certainly the "mastermind", John Shelbury, "The answers I have drafted, Mr Harriot, are not very informative but they will keep you out of trouble and not damage Sir Walter's case" We have discussed

Harriot's spinning of his account of the Roanoke settlement in favour of his master's campaign for American colonisation:[23] for this he would probably have been regarded by contemporaries as loyal rather than dishonest. The same conclusion emerges from his unfortunate involvements in the witchhunt against Ralegh's "atheism" and in the political fall-out from the Gunpowder Plot.[24] It is significant, too, that while Harriot faithfully continued to serve Ralegh until his death he did not decline Northumberland's offer to make him a "gentleman pensioner", giving him a secure life at Syon House to pursue his real interests. Harriot was not interested in politics, as he stated publicly, nor, it may be presumed, in criminal activities or in ruining Sanderson. By the time that he presented his petition to Star Chamber Sanderson had gathered detailed information about the forgery – why it was thought necessary; who had arranged it; how William Meere had delivered the actual document and took the "fee", in order to distance his father John Meere, who was the obvious candidate for forger – after all, he had done it before, and so on; so it seems obvious that he had obtained inside information, at a time when he himself was already in a debtor's prison. Despite this, Sanderson displayed his customary energy, he somehow found the necessary resources, and he was not without friends and well-wishers. In the years between 1585 and 1595, when he served as Raleigh's Honorary Treasurer, Sanderson must have been welcomed by the Ralegh household as, at the very least, a stabilising influence in the turbulent life of their employer. It is possible, in addition, that his commercial and financial skill and honesty were also noticed. While there is no direct evidence on the point it may be suggested that Harriot was the insider who fed the information about the forgery to Sanderson; bearing in mind that it was Harriot who had examined Sanderson's accounts on behalf of Ralegh. If there was anything suspicious or questionable, he must have obtained explanations from Sanderson, and the release was presumably drawn up and executed **because Harriot was satisfied with the accounts**[25]. Harriot's interrogatories 5 and 6, in which he claimed that there was nothing falsified in the said account and that the dealings of both men were honourable.[26] It is significant, too, see below, that Sanderson did not include Harriot, or the second administrator (Robert Smith), in the list of individuals whom he asked Star Chamber to interrogate.

Ralegh writes to the Judge

On 19th June 1611 Ralegh wrote from the Tower to the judge hearing his case against Sanderson and the latter's counterclaim, Sir Edward Phelips. While published with useful notes in the 1999 edition of Youings, the letter appears not to have been considered by scholars concentrating on the Ralegh/Sanderson story.[27]

As mentioned above such correspondence was not unusual in the 16th century, and, for example, Ralegh wrote several letters to magistrates and ministers trying to get John Meere imprisoned. To-day such conduct would be punished as contempt of Court

While it has been suggested that Ralegh may have helped Phelips become MP of Penrhyn,[28] the letter indicates that, on this occasion, at least, Ralegh was not seeking a return for past favours; so we have simply a private letter from Ralegh trying to further his own ends. We have seen that the prime objective of Ralegh and his legal team was to establish the release to Sanderson as conditional, not absolute; in order to persuade the Court to order re-accounting for the years to 1595, and then to let the matter get bogged down, run up costs &c., in hope that the counterclaim for £4,000 can be delayed and perhaps finally smothered

Sure enough, the second sentence in Ralegh's letter reads "Before the Commission was sent[29] it was proved by Mr Heriots oath that my release to Sanderson was but conditionale, aye, his owne borrowing of it for certain days to show his creditors, and his restoring of it to Heriot agayne, did sufficiently prove it". Apart from this sentence there does not appear to be any suggestion in the surviving documents that Sanderson had "borrowed" the release to show his creditors (under the pseudo-legal "decree" pronounced by Ralegh at Plympton) and then returned it. Indeed, Sanderson stated in his "answer" i.e. his defence in the Chancery action, that he had tried to get the release from Harriot but to no avail and had "recently" seen it in his hands (presumably in 1611). Harriot was vague about his unbroken possession of the release over 16 years, but he never stated that Sanderson had "borrowed it back" to explain matters to his creditors, as might have been expected if this had happened. The purpose of Ralegh's sentence is not clear, and it is hard to make any meaningful connection between "Sanderson's borrowing back" and "Heriots oath". What is clear that if Sanderson was driven to borrow the release to fend off his creditors and then in due course returned it to Harriot, in accordance with Ralegh's "decrees" (i) this did not mean that Sanderson had agreed to the "decrees" (ii) this would not alter the legal effect of the release document; whether it was absolute or conditional would depend on its wording and the Court's interpretation of such wording.

Further, if Ralegh succeeded in persuading the Judge that Sanderson had borrowed and returned the release, whether or not this had actually happened, he might be fatally damaging his own case. The borrowing must have taken place at some time in the sixteen years between 1595 and the trial in May 1611. On this basis, when Sanderson obtained the release from

Harriot he would have seen whether or not the endorsement had been added. If it had, he would not have remained silent, still less have quietly returned the document to Harriot. If it had not, he would in due course have returned it to Harriot: but when the release with an endorsement was finally produced to the Court, he would not merely have denounced it as a forgery – he would have said that "The endorsement has been added since I last saw the document in 15XX." Ralegh's case was that the endorsement was part of the original document; but by establishing that Sanderson had seen the release at some time during the 16 year period he would have fatally undermined it.

It is important to note that the letter was written after the Commission had returned from administering interrogatories; so Ralegh will have heard this from his solicitor, John Shelbury, that he (Shelbury) had "weeded" the interrogatories so that the ones dealing with the endorsement alleged to have been forged had not been put to the witnesses, and that Chritopher Harris had died before swearing any interrogatories; effectively, that no evidence had been found to support Sanderson's allegation of forgery. Knowing this, Ralegh seems to have concluded that it was timely to try to steer the judge towards accepting that, in the absence of any additional evidence of forgery, the suspect endorsement was genuine, and that, in consequence, the release was conditional after all. If that involved stating or suggesting, falsely, that Sanderson had borrowed back the release, so be it. When under pressure Ralegh was accustomed to abandon the truth.
Apart from conditionality, there are some detailed points in the letter – apparently on the connection between the claim for re-accounting and the counterclaim for a money payment, and the letter follows Ralegh's usual practice: – one or two insults "the unchristian sute" and "this pernicious miscreant", and two allegations, one of bribery and the other of improper receipt of money

The result, when the case came back to court in November 1611 was that no further evidence of forgery had been obtained, and Ralegh's team (Sanderson called them "the confederators" i.e. conspirators) again maintained that the endorsement was genuine. The inconclusive investigation of the forgery further delayed matters in the Chancery Court, so that seems to be why Sanderson turned to Star Chamber, which was authorised to hear criminal matters like forgery, only to be met there by the specious objection from Ralegh's team that Star Chamber should not hear the case until the Chancery suit had been disposed of.

Star Chamber

We now describe these proceedings. They were not by way of appeal, the Star Chamber having its own separate jurisdiction, including crime and maladministration, which were outside the scope of the Chancery Court. The main reason for Sanderson's petition to Star Chamber (in 1613) was the failure of the Chancery Court, for the reasons already explained, to investigate the issue of the forgery. Star Chamber could move directly to examine those who, he maintained, had conspired to ruin him by forgery, perjury and tampering with court documents ; but he had other grievances too. He started by explaining his relationship with Raleigh and his management of his affairs without any payment, and how he brought in at least £30,000 which Raleigh could never have raised on his own. He then moved on to Raleigh's conviction for high treason and consequent attainder and the appointment[30] of the "administrators" (Shelbury and Smith) "upon confidence and trust that [they] should satisfy and pay the debts of the said Sir Walter Raleigh". However, "Contrary. to the said trust....and by the direction of the said Sir Walter Raleigh" the administrators commenced the Chancery proceedings against Sanderson".[31] He then described the Plymstock episode, mentioning the £1,600 or £1,700 borrowed by him on his own account and made over to Raleigh. He maintained that the administrators had raised some £6,000 but had "contrary to all equity and confidence" refused to pay the debts owed to Sanderson. He then returned to the Chancery action explaining how, as the evidence appeared to be counting against Ralegh's case, the forgery was hatched to defraud him of his counterclaims and "whereby the release made by [Ralegh] to [Sanderson] might be avoided". He also reported Shelbury's tampering with the interrogatories in order to suppress evidence of the forgery. He then stated that Ralegh's team had again protested the validity of the endorsement at the hearing in November 1611 and mentioned that he had on that occasion spotted the erroneous use of Gwyana in a document purporting to have been prepared in January/February 1595. He therefore asked for writs of subpoena to be served on Raleigh, John Meere, John Shelbury and William Meere (but not, be it noted, Thomas Harriot or Robert Smith) for them to appear and answer his charges.

We must now stand back and address the two important questions (i) Why were the proceedings in the Chancery Court started? (ii) What was the outcome of the litigation, both in Chancery and Star Chamber?

Sanderson's petition to Star Chamber states that the Chancery proceedings were started when he asked the administrators to pay him the money owed by Raleigh. The proceedings, based on the conditions "imposed" by Raleigh in January/February 1595, could, assuming the validity of those conditions, have been commenced at any time after Raleigh's return from Guyana in August/September 1595. We have suggested that Sanderson had refrained from demanding payment earlier out of misplaced trust in Raleigh's promises to pay and because he decided to maintain friendship (or a show of friendship) between the two families. We do not know why he changed his mind and demanded payment, but the most likely explanations are either (i) he was being himself pressed by his own creditors from whom he had borrowed (back in 1594 or 1595) the £1,600 or £1,700 to repay these sums plus the penalties and interest which had accrued in the meantime, or (ii) having paid off the £1,600/£1,700 loans plus interest, penalties &c., and having received no reimbursement from Raleigh, he had since become involved in some other financial crisis and needed to call in all money owed to him. The latter explanation is more likely.

Whatever the reason for Sanderson's belated demand for reimbursement, the commencement of proceedings against him in Raleigh's name does look like the delivery of the long prepared pre-emptive strike. When we considered[32] why Raleigh had staged the unilateral retrospective imposition of conditions at Plymstock in 1595 we suggested that this was the most likely reason. Sixteen years later, it seems, Raleigh decided to spring the trap.[33]

Explaining the outcome of the litigation, in the absence of court records as to what happened, also requires a hypothesis based on what is most likely. The original Chancery proceedings were weakly based, the plaintiffs produced a document which, in itself, looked suspicious, and Sanderson, in Star Chamber, offered positive evidence of forgery (as well as of other wrongdoing). If the two cases had proceeded to judgment, it looks likely that (i) the plaint in Chancery would have been dismissed (ii) Sanderson's counterclaim would have been upheld (iii) Star Chamber would have established a conspiracy to forge and defraud Sanderson (iv) the conspirators (including Raleigh) would have been convicted and punished (v) Shelbury's career as a solicitor would have come to an abrupt end . It seems reasonable to conclude that the likelihood of these painful results was enough to convince Ralegh to call off his claim to have Sanderson's accounts re-opened. On this hypothesis, what was Sanderson to do? While it beggars belief, it looks as though, once more, he considered it best not to press his counterclaim and not to pursue Raleigh and his henchmen in Star Chamber. Perhaps, once again, Ralegh made promises about the debts being paid and played the family card. A simpler explanation might be that Sanderson had by then run out of money and could not afford to continue the proceedings. Whatever the true reasons, we might therefore conclude that the actions were simply discontinued. However unlikely this scenario appears, it does account for what happened and for what failed to happen. Needless to say, Raleigh and his "administrators" never paid Sanderson's debts. If they had, the cash would have enabled Sanderson to escape from debtors' prison, where he was held because he owed comparatively small sums.[34] According to the ODNB 2004 account Sanderson only got his money back by going to law after Raleigh's execution in 1618; though no evidence of this has yet been found, and Sanderson did not get out of debtors' prison until 1622 – and then not by paying his creditor, but by persuading the Lord Chancellor in the Chancery Court that he had already paid more than he really owed.[35].

15

Debtors' Prisons

We must now return to look at what had been happening to Sanderson apart from the 1611 litigation. We have already described, with tantalisingly scant detail, his involvement in farming the Mines Royal. This, we are told by Sir William in An Answer occurred under James I i.e. at some time after 1603. We are told, too, that he put many men to work on the mining operations and made large losses. Our next positive evidence, apart from the unfolding of the 1611 litigation, is the record of his borrowing from a moneylender and his imprisonment for debt.

In 1612 Sanderson borrowed £100 from a well-known moneylender "George Pitt, Citizen and barber-surgeon but at that time using the trade of a dyer". To secure the repayment plus interest after six months, Sanderson and his son Raleigh Sanderson (almost certainly his eldest son and therefore his heir) entered into a recognisance in the sum of £200.[1]

Pitt appears to have granted an extension to the original six months period – because further claims had been made against Sanderson, probably from his disastrous investment in mining. About this time Pitt had obtained, probably by purchase, appointment as Usher to the Chancery Court: this gave him the privilege of being sued only in that court – a considerable advantage to an active moneylender. Pitt then, without informing Sanderson, obtained judgment on the £200 recognisance, plus a writ of execution, so that the Sheriff of Middlesex seized goods in Sanderson's house at Islington to that value. Sanderson claimed that, about this time he had paid £70 to Pitt in hope of having the recognisance cancelled.

In 1613 Sanderson was arrested for separate debts, based on guarantee liabilities, of around £450 and was imprisoned in the house of the Deputy Bailiff of the Liberty of Westminster. Pitt agreed to lend this sum for nine months against a mortgage of Sanderson's house/tavern in Lower Thames Street, the Golden Hoope, which yielded rent of about £64 p.a. It was agreed that the same solicitor would act for both parties. Around 11th March Pitt called at the deputy Bailiff's house with the mortgage deed and bags of money. Stating that he was in a hurry to reach his office, Pitt persuaded Sanderson to execute the mortgage deed, without it being checked and without counting the cash. Pitt then announced that the bags contained only £350 and that he would bring the balance of £100 within about a week. On counting the cash Sanderson found that it was "a good parte short of £350". Despite many applications Pitt refused (i) to deliver the shortfall (ii) to deliver the £100 (iii) to acknowledge that the recognisance had been satisfied. Pitt maintained that Sanderson had agreed to pay him the amount of the deficieny i.e £100 + £20 "shortfall".

Shortly afterwards Sanderson was again arrested for other guarantee liabilities. Pitt still did not pay the money he owed (shortfall + £100); retained possession of the Golden Hoope to cover the mortgage interest; was trying to acquire the freehold for half its true value and was threatening to apply for a new writ of execution on the original £200 recognisance. Sanderson was unable to proceed against Pitt at common law because of his special position as Chancery Usher,[2] and as he did not have any spare cash, he remained imprisoned for around eight years (until 1622) first in the Fleet and later in the Westminster Gatehouse. The debts for which he remained imprisoned were comparatively small, so that payment by Ralegh (or his administrators) of only part of what Sanderson said he owed would have enabled Sanderson to obtain his liberty.

Sanderson therefore petitioned the Lord Chancellor in the Chancery court on 22nd May 1620 to examine Pitt on his complaint.

In his answer Pitt contested most of the allegations mentioned above, in particular that the £100 and the £20 "shortfall" were owing to Sanderson. Pitt maintained that Sanderson had agreed to pay him the £120 and stated that he had lent Sanderson a further £10 in 1615, a further £5 in 1616 and a further £6 to Mrs Sanderson in 1618. Pitt revealed that Sanderson had sold the house next door to the Golden Hoope to one Camarthen (sometimes Camarden, probably a relation of Sanderson by marriage) and that he (Pitt) had bought it from Camarthen for £373 3s. Finally, Pitt maintained that he was still owed £903 14s. and should either be paid this sum or have the Golden Hoope transferred to him.

There are no further records of Sanderson's case. It looks as though he succeeded in having the Golden Hoope mortgage discharged as well as recovering his personal liberty in 1622. Within a short time of being released Sanderson was appointed, with other well-qualified people (including his fellow mercantilist Gerard Malynes), to a Committee established by the Privy Council to inquire into problems of foreign exchange and trade credit affecting the export of English woollen cloth.

A few comments may be offered:-

(i) Sanderson's unbusinesslike behaviour on the execution of the mortgage suggests that his characteristic commercial acumen had disappeared under the pressure of his money problems.

(ii) At the time there was no general system of bankruptcy, with an orderly allocation of assets to meet liabilities by a public official supervised by the court. The 1571 Bankrupts Act applied only to traders and craftsmen and all other insolvent debtors had to wait for a change in the law until 1861; so they had either to pay up or risk imprisonment for debt. There were complicated legal rules involved and this cruel and ineffective state of affairs remained a blot on the English legal sytem for three hundred years, despite repeated efforts to introduce reform.

(iii) In 1620 Sanderson had attempted to borrow £50 from the Fishmongers' Company against the security of some "mappes". This was refused.[3]

(iv) It will be noted that Sanderson's imprisonment for debt was obtained by two creditors in respect of guarantee or surety liabilities, not by the moneylender Pitt. The latter used a recognisance on the first debt, on which he obtained judgment and seizure of goods, and for the second debt he relied on a mortgage on one of the Sanderson family houses in Thames Street (see below).

(v) Pitt's moneylending activities were investigated by the Attorney General in 1633.

(vi) Sanderson had sold "the house next door to the Golden Hoope" to Richard Camarden (probably a relation by marriage) for £322 in March 1606. He also sold a freehold orchard at Lambeth for £40 in October 1606. These may have been part of Sanderson's efforts to raise cash to meet the debts resulting from his mining obligations

Part Four
Judgement Deferred

16

End of the Story?

Ralegh died on the scaffold in 1618, the Sanderson family having visited him in prison the previous night; Sanderson himself was at this time in a debtors' prison and would have had to obtain permission to visit his uncle-in-law.

Sanderson escaped from prison only in 1622 (aged around 74) by successfully petitioning the Lord Chancellor to the effect that he had already paid all that he really owed.[1]

Sanderson seems to have passed the last 16 years of his long life living quietly "in the Strand", with the family property portfolio largely intact but everything else gone. He died in 1638, with 16 instalments of "quarterage" owing to the Fishmongers' Company. His body was embalmed to await the return of his surviving sons from overseas to bury him in "the parish church of the Savoy".[2]

Bess Ralegh embarked on a long-term plan (i) to boost (or restore) Ralegh's reputation – depending on one's point of view – following his courageous stance on the scaffold (ii) to recover money and property to which Ralegh was entitled, or to which she felt he was entitled, and (iii) to have Carew Ralegh "restored in blood and lands" from the effect of his father's attainder. Bess employed Ralegh's team of John Shelbury and John Meere for the legal work.

The relationship between Ralegh and Sanderson thus ended in 1618. Was this the end of the story? Not quite: there is one more chapter to be considered and then we must proceed to judgment.

The Drama Replayed

First, some 38 years later the Ralegh/Sanderson drama was re-played – on paper, as part of a literary spat between Sir William and an anonymous writer. In the course of 1656 (i) Sir William wrote a "History of Queen Mary of Scotland and her son James VI/ I" (ii) an anonymous writer (variously identified as Carew Ralegh, Ralegh's surviving son; another writer provided with ammunition by Carew Ralegh, or as Peter Helyn: see further Appendix A) in "Observations" took exception to a number of statements in the History, a few being about Ralegh's trial and one to the effect that Ralegh had no knowledge of a definite gold mine in Guyana in 1616. The criticisms were "spiced up", but in no way strengthened, by offensive personal invective against (a) Sir William as the author (b) his wife Dame Bridget and (c) his father Sanderson. (iii) Sir William published "An Answer" defending the character and conduct of his wife, his father and of himself. This gave us the lively biographical notes on Sanderson which have been used throughout this book.[3]

The literary re-play does not, in the event, change the story told in this book; since (i) the Observations criticised many statements in the History (ii) these criticisms, or some of them, may well have been valid – Sir William has never been highly regarded as a historian.(iii) the gratuitous abuse of the author, his wife and father had no bearing whatever on the criticised statements (iv) While Sir William deals separately with the historical criticisms, his biographical notes in "An Answer" concerning himself, his wife and his father are directed to rebutting the abuse. It is important to keep the two sets of issues separate, and to recognise (a) that Sir William, as a mediocre historian, may still tell the truth about his family (b) that there is no particular reason why an anonymous "Seeker after Truth" who is trying to rubbish a historical book should have any knowledge of the character and conduct of the author, his wife or his father.

It is therefore timely to draw together the important aspects of the Ralegh-Sanderson relationship, define the significant issues and strive to provide convincing answers or explanations.

17

Final Verdict

Having gathered all the information about the Ralegh/Sanderson relationship we have to "make sense" of it. Everyone who starts on the story soon stumbles on reading about the Plymstock Incident. How could Ralegh – apparently to save paying around £2000 which he owed, when his income was £8–10 thousand p.a., destroy a treasurership and banking arrangement which cost nothing, which had already run successfully for some 10 years, with a City merchant of great ability who enjoyed "undoubted credit", who was happily married to his niece, in a dishonest and humiliating way?

If that is hard to credit, Sanderson's reaction is perhaps harder still. When he had recovered his temper his first reaction was one of regret that he had not bidden farewell to the uncle-in-law, whom he seems to have idolised, who was setting off for South America with a fair chance of not returning alive – Ralegh was due to board his ship within hours of Sanderson storming out of Sir Christopher Harris' house. In September of 1595 Sanderson sends his nephew John Janes, bearing a private letter, to Lord Burleigh to corroborate Ralegh's story, for which Ralegh had been ridiculed, about native South Americans who had dog faces or wore masks simulating dog faces. We have no positive evidence that Ralegh and Sanderson met in the period between 1595 and 1603, when Sanderson organised the party of horsemen to show respect and support on Hounslow Heath – though from the context they must have done Once Ralegh was in the Tower Sanderson was active in supporting Bess' request to join her husband, and the Sandersons visited regularly en famille. The list of acts of loyalty and support goes on and only ends the night before Ralegh's execution in 1618, when Sanderson took his family to visit him in prison.

In view of the inherent improbability of Sanderson's loyalty surviving the Plymstock Incident, the present writer's initial view was that Sanderson and his family were merely putting on a show of maintaining amicable relations for public consumption. Further consideration, however, has suggested that Sanderson's loyalty, if "obstinate", was indeed genuine. The three main arguments were (i) the ongoing list of Sanderson's acts of respect and support (ii) the fact that the demonstrations of undiminished loyalty were recorded by Sir William, even though he clearly saw Ralegh in a less favourable light than his father did (iii) the fact that Sanderson, in his petition to Star Chamber, despite the Plymstock humiliation and, more recently, the forged endorsement and the tampering with the interrogatories, still felt able to describe how he met Ralegh, following his marriage to Ralegh's niece, " by means of which intermarriage your subject and Sir Walter Raleigh became acquainted and grew into inward love and friendship…" The only possible lapse in loyalty occurred when Sanderson, desperate for funds after his mining crash, in 1611 finally made formal demand for reimbursement, not indeed from Ralegh personally, but from the "administrators" appointed, under Crown authority, to pay his debts: this of course triggered the Chancery action for re-accounting which we have described.

We can only speculate as to the basis for the obstinate loyalty – controversial opinions and attitudes are usually derived from several causes. Sanderson seems to have hero worshipped Ralegh and, no doubt, enjoyed the reflected glory from the best known man in England. Almost certainly, from the outset, he would have regarded Ralegh as being of superior "rank" Mrs Sanderson, too, may have influenced him. Further, the pride of a successful merchant who is also wealthy may have convinced Sanderson that he can rise above the loss of £4000 (say £500,000 to-day) and disregard the shabby charade composed by a sharp lawyer for Ralegh to perform.

We can now therefore turn to consider the following:-

The Issues

1. Why did friendship between the two men, following Sanderson's marriage, ever develop into a professional commercial/financial collaboration? They could have remained kinsmen by marriage and good friends.

2. Why did this collaboration collapse in 1595?

3. Why did Sanderson continue to treat Ralegh with respect and make efforts to support and assist the Ralegh family?

4. What verdicts should be passed on the litigation commencing in 1611 between the two men?

5. On a broader, moral plane, "Who was in the right?" and "Who was in the wrong?"

Issue 1 – The Professional Collaboration

Once we strip out the bitter sarcasm (about penniless, unscrupulous courtiers) of Sir William who, with his younger siblings and perhaps also his mother, had good reason to regret Sanderson's financial link with Ralegh, it is tolerably clear that Ralegh and Sanderson collaborated on money matters because it was a mutually attractive idea. Ralegh saw a wealthy young merchant who had established himself in the Northern European market and had already achieved a good reputation in the City, who shared his patriotism, had a knowledge of ships and navigation, and who could, as his "man of business" or treasurer, financially manage the meteoric rise to fame and fortune which he planned for himself. Sanderson was obviously swept off his feet by the charm, presence, abilities and boundless confidence of England's rising man par excellence; marrying the niece of such a man was definite social advancement for a City man (however "worshipful"), being linked with him in his imperial projects would be a bonus, and would in itself fulfil his own ambition to do something for England. At the same time he saw little financial risk with the substantial cash benefits being steered towards Ralegh by the Queen.

We noted at the outset the disparity in "rank" between the two men. This in no way conflicted with the mutual advantages presented to them, but it appears that, from the start, Sanderson "looked up to" his younger uncle-in-law, displaying a loyalty as absolute as that displayed by other members of Ralegh's household or "circle" like Thomas Harriot and Lawrence Keymis. It is suggested that consciousness of rank, allied with kinship by marriage, was a central thread in Sanderson's relationship with Ralegh.

Issue 2 – The Plymstock Incident

When attempting to analyse the falling-out, we suggested that, in the first instance, Ralegh, by discouraging a settlement of accounts, was trying to keep Sanderson "on a string" for future use; and then, either because Sanderson persisted or because his advisers though it would be advantageous, accepted the idea of a settlement – only to find that mutual releases had the opposite effect, "wiping out" all previous transactions but crystalising the £2,000 owing to Sanderson. The "escape route" designed by the lawyers was to convert the absolute release which Ralegh granted into a conditional release, with retrospective effect – but the decision to follow it was obviously Ralegh's own. We concluded that Ralegh decided that he would not pay, either then or subsequently. the £2000 (which over time grew to £4000 because of interest and penalty payments) and was indifferent as to (i) whether or not he lost Sanderson's services as a result and (ii) whether or not this ruined Sanderson. The most likely reason was that, after 10 or 11 years Ralegh felt he could manage his finances without Sanderson's help.

Seeing that Ralegh had never rewarded Sanderson for an apparently faultless performance over the previous 10 or 11 years, the most charitable thing that can be said of his decision is that it was typical of the man – a flaw in a complex and contradictory character. Alternatively, we can agree with Sanderson and describe Ralegh's conduct as dishonest and wicked. It would be difficult to devise a more offensive insult to Sanderson's loyalty and his standing as a leading London merchant than (i) "stealing back" the release document (with all the supporting evidence) (ii) having Ralegh make a pseudo-legal declaration, purporting to vary in his favour the rights which he had granted a few days earlier, and (iii) requiring Sanderson to defer to a much younger employee of Ralegh's if he wished to make use of the release document which Ralegh had voluntarily handed to him.

Issue 3 – Sanderson's "obstinate loyalty"

We have tried to analyse and explain this above[1], concluding that it was, perhaps, a blend of consciousness of rank; hero worship and the pride of a successful, wealthy "Worshipful Citizen and Fishmonger"

Issue 4 – The Litigation

While we have no positive evidence of the actual outcome of either case, in the Chancery Court or in Star Chamber, we can, with some confidence, suggest what would have happened if the cases had proceeded to judgment

4.1.The Chancery Court
4.1.1. Ralegh's claim for full re-accounting would have been dismissed as "stale", on the grounds of 16 years unexplained delay (See the detailed analysis at p. 101ff.)

4.1.2. Sanderson's counterclaim might, ironically, have been resisted on the same grounds; since it could have been argued that he might have sued at any time after the mutual releases in 1595 established that he was owed money. However, the equitable principle was at *unexplained* delay could defeat a claim in Chancery, and Sanderson could have given evidence about Ralegh's protestations on Hounslow Heath, and, as we have suggested, other occasions as well, as establishing that Ralegh intended to pay up when he was in a position to do so. So it is tolerably clear that judgment would have been given upholding the counterclaim for the £4000 sum.

4.2. Star Chamber

On the evidence which Sanderson offered, the Court would have had no difficulty, after examining the parties named by Sanderson – Ralegh himself, Shelbury, John Meere and his son (but not, be it noted, Harriot or Robert Smith) – in finding a conspiracy to ruin his reputation and cause him financial loss by forging the endorsement on the 1595 release and tampering with Court documents, the interrogatories ordered by the Master of the Rolls to investigate the circumstances surrounding the challenged endorsement.

4.3. What actually happened with the litigation?.

It looks as though both cases were abandoned. With Sanderson in a strong, if not commanding, position how could that be? A facile answer – which could be neither proved nor disproved – would be that, following his financial crash, he had no funds to carry on. It is suggested, however, that this is not the right answer. Sanderson, after being thwarted in the Chancery Court, found the funds to bring a suit in Star Chamber, and later, somehow found the funds to successfully petition the Lord Chancellor to release him from a debtor's prison. He also raised £450 by mortgaging his house in Thames Street (though he was apparently tricked into receiving a smaller sum) to pay off additional.claims that came in from the mining disaster, and he had other valuable properties on which he could have raised more had he wished to do so.[2] A more likely explanation is that his obstinate loyalty to Ralegh. which runs all through their relationship and produced some scarcely believable results, like his continuing to help and support the Raleghs after his humiliation at Plymstock, prevented him from pursuing his legal rights.[3]

On Ralegh's side, if he had pressed on in the Chancery Court his claim for re-accounting would have been rejected and judgment would have been given in Sanderson's favour on his counterclaim. On the analysis which we have presented, The Master of the Rolls would not have needed to pronounce on the forgery issue, just as the judge did not need to do in Bess' case against the jeweller van Lore in 1625.

We cannot know whether abandonment was mutually agreed between the parties or their representatives; but, in view of the bizarre parallel relationships – cordial social intercourse on the one hand and bitter accusations and counter-accusations in the Courts on the other – it is quite possible that some understanding was worked out.

Issue 5. The Moral High Ground

The three issues here are (i) Was Sanderson an effective and honest treasurer? (ii) Ralegh's behaviour at Plymstock and (iii) Ralegh's behaviour subsequently.

(i) We know that Sanderson worked as treasurer and banker for no reward, for about ten years. He stated that there had been no complaints while he was doing the work and this was not challenged. When cash was short he used his own credit to borrow or put in his own money. He committed his own ships to the efforts to relieve the Roanoke Settlement. As to honesty, Harriot scrutinised, questioned and passed his accounts. Two allegations were made against Sanderson's accounts: first, that they were too general and, secondly, that £60,000 was insufficiently accounted for. In view of Harriot's approval and Ralegh's release these cannot stand

(ii) The only possible justification for Ralegh's behaviour would have been if some fraud or dishonesty of Sanderson had been discovered after Harriott's audit and Ralegh's release – but this was not the case. At best, therefore, his behaviour was cynical and, at worst, downright wicked.

(iii) While we speculated[4] that Ralegh's policy was "sweet words and promises to pay – but if he makes formal demand for payment, then sue him for re-accounting" we do not know enough to pass a moral judgment.over the long period involved.

Opinions and Judgments to date

Any "appellate court" has the advantage of being able to study and consider what has gone before – much of the ground-breaking work has been done. Until the far-ranging article on Sanderson by Ruth McIntyre in 1956 there had been no examination of his collaboration with Ralegh, and writers seem to have frequently confused Sanderson and Sir William.[5]

It is convenient to mention here two 19th century criticisms of Sanderson's performance as treasurer to his uncle-in-law, made by Edward Edwards in his biography of Ralegh[6] and by Henry Stevens in his biography of Thomas Harriot.[7] Edwards says, " He was not more fortunate in the case of his own kinsman, William Sanderson (the husband of Margaret Snedale, Sir Walter's niece), who fell heavily in arrears, when afterwards administering the same office" i.e the "Wine Licensing Office". Stevens made similar criticisms. It is striking that neither biographer offers any source for these quite serious allegations, and it looks as though both are derived (directly or indirectly) from a passage in "Observations" where the anonymous author, the self-styled "Lover of Truth", is not criticising Sir William's historical writing but is heaping personal abuse on Sanderson as well as his son and daughter-in-law. For a number of reasons it is suggested that these allegations cannot stand.[8]

We must now collect and consider the "verdicts" pronounced (or not pronounced) by commentators over the last 60 years on the legal and moral issues between Ralegh and Sanderson. Before doing that, however, we must recall that we have available the contemporary evidence of a reliable expert witness.

The Expert Witness

No one has challenged the evidence of Thomas Harriot, the "auditor", either at the time or since. After studying Sanderson's accounts, and asking him questions, Harriot concluded that he had fully accounted for all the cash which had passed through his hands while he acted as Ralegh's treasurer. Harriot was reckoned one of the cleverest men of his time, and he was (among many other things) a consummate mathematician, experienced in managing Ralegh's financial affairs; nor has anyone, either at the time or since, challenged his integrity. The efforts of Ralegh.s legal team were all directed to showing that Ralegh's absolute release to Sanderson was, contrary to its clear terms, not absolute but conditional, a hopeless and undedifying task. Even if they had succeeded, this would not have affected the validity of the audit certificate and, as we have endeavoured to explain, the end result (had the cases proceeded to judgment) would have been the same.

In 1949 Dr John Shirley concluded[9] "All the extant evidence is before the reader, and it is he who must assume the role of judge in the controversy between Sir Walter Raleigh, Knight and William Sanderson, gent."

In 1956 Dr.Ruth McIntyre was sympathetic to Sanderson, stating "He had learned no doubt, that serving a courtier was an expensive proposition, even though the courtier had fallen from grace". However, she recalled the objective of her important article – Sanderson's contribution as a financier of discovery – and went on to comment, "We should like to know more about this unhappy part of Sanderson's career and how he rehabilitated himself, but except for the fact that the suits at law grew out of late sixteenth – century maritime ventures, his legal and financial difficulties have no direct bearing on the history of overseas expansion".

By 1983, in his definitive biography of Thomas Harriot, Dr John Shirley (at p.222) had advanced beyond his 1949 "leave it to the reader" position to state "Whether Ralegh was devious in the handling of his finances, whether he would stoop to forgery and perjury as well as deceit was not settled by the court. Whether Sanderson was a victim of false practices, or was himself a conniving financier, bringing suit against those he owed in an attempt to avoid just payment, cannot be determined. Probably the truth lay somewhere in between with two sharp operators using the courts for their own purposes, and the go-between, Harriot, refusing clear statements about his own activities, avoiding personal trouble by verbal evasions". It is suggested that the line of reasoning is unfair to Sanderson for the following reasons (i) "Whether Sanderson…was himself a connivng financier, bringing suit….cannot be determined". Sanderson did not "bring suit" – in the Chancery Court he counter-claimed in Ralegh's proceedings for the money he said Ralegh had taken for the El Dorado voyage and had not repaid; and, in bringing suit in Star Chamber, he was complaining about matters for which there was much evidence. Neither set of allegations by Sanderson, it is suggested, makes him "a conniving financier" (ii) "two sharp operators using the courts for their own purposes". As explained above (see p. 100), Ralegh's allegation was probably not of fraud, but of "insufficient accounting", and, in any case, no evidence was offered that Sanderson was "a sharp operator": Indeed, Ralegh's team commented on his meticulous recording of all cash transactions, both receipts and disbursements.

In 1997 Rosalind Davies published Occasional Paper No.24 in the Durham Thomas Harriot Seminar series[10]. Being primarily focussed on Harriot, the Paper stresses (p.8) that Harriot's role as auditor was independent and agreed by all parties; that to his knowledge there was nothing falsified in the accounts; and that both men had dealt honourably; with regard to the alleged forgery of the endorsement (p.9), that he had not changed anything in the deed of release but could not be certain that no one else had. Next the view is expressed that Harriot knowingly assisted Ralegh both in doing down Sanderson (p.18. "The significance of Ralegh's and Harriot's financial duplicity is attested by the weight which Ralegh gave to the definition of profit and expenditure in the *Discoverie* itself"); in misrepresenting the voyage as a chivalrous discovery, undertaking by Ralegh at his own cost, preparing Guiana as an offering to the Queen (instead of pillaging it) and therefore trying to have the country reserved for future development by Ralegh, safe from the greedy exploitation of other Englishmen (p.19). On the argument in favour of forgery based on the use of the name "Gwyana", the Paper says, "The veracity of William Sanderson' claim that the word 'Guiana' was not known until Ralegh brought it home in September 1595 is hard to disprove, as before and after 1595, maps show the region variously as 'Paria' and 'Caribana' "

On the misrepresentation of the nature of the first Guiana expedition and the effort to make it a Ralegh "sphere of influence" it is suggested that Harriot going along with what his employer wants was, in 16th century terms, loyalty rather than reprehensible conduct, similar to his spinning of the Brief and True Account of the new found land of Virginia (see above p. 49). Forgery and tampering with court documents are more serious matters but we have tried to show (see p. 100 above) that Harriot was put in an impossible position by his employer.

In 1999 Ralegh's Letters, edited by Agnes Latham and Joyce Youings, were published. Letter 204 was written in June 1611 by Ralegh to the Master of the Rolls, who was in the middle of trying Ralegh's action in the Chancery Court against Sanderson.(For the text of the letter see Appendix F, and for comment on what Ralegh was trying to achieve by writing to the judge, see above p. 111). In May 1611 Sanderson sued Ralegh and his team in Star Chamber alleging that they had conspired to ruin him by (i) forging an endorsement on the deed of release which Ralegh had issued to Sanderson in 1595 after Harriot had audited and approved the accounts which Sanderson had submitted, covering some eight or more years prior to 1595; and submitting the forged document to the Chancery Court (ii) altering court documents in the Chancery proceedings so as to suppress evidence of the forgery. Commenting on the two cases (in Chancery and Star Chamber) the editors state "The judgments of neither court are on record. If one might hazard a guess on the basis of the surviving evidence it would be that neither party obtained satisfaction and that this was an equitable outcome, there being little to choose between them for vexatious litigation". In English legal phraseology a "vexatious litigant" is a person who commences a number of proceedings **based on the same claim**, and to-day there are arrangements in place under which such a litigant can be prevented from starting additional proceedings – on the basis that they are a waste of time and money. The matters litigated in the Chancery Court had not been the subject of prior legal proceedings, and the matters of which Sanderson complained in Star Chamber (while arising out of the dispute in Chancery) were different, being allegations of criminal offences, over which Star Chamber had jurisdiction.; and of which there certainly was evidence Perhaps, therefore, "vexatious litigation" is intended here to mean something different. However, the claim for re-accounting and the counterclaim for reimbursement of monies obtained by Sanderson for Ralegh's use, in the Chancery Court, and Sanderson's request for investigation of alleged crimes in Star Chamber, are sufficiently described in the surviving documents to be evaluated – and it is hard to see how an exactly balanced 50/50 result can be deduced.

Again in 1999, Professor Theodore Leinhard published Theatre, Finance and Society in Early Modern England. He has some interesting comments (pp.116–7) "Affiliation may be more precisely described as manipulation when a courtly adventurer like Ralegh tricks a financier like William Sanderson into returning to him the 'Acquittance and Release' Ralegh had given him prior to setting sail for Guiana in 1595. Sanderson had good reason to believe that if either of them owed the other anything, it was Ralegh who was still in debt to Sanderson. But without Ralegh's release in hand (it had been given to Thomas Harriot, ostensibly for safe keeping) Sanderson was later to find himself fighting from a precarious perch – a debtor in the Fleet – with those among Ralegh's friends who had been granted the administration of his estate following his attainder. Suits over financial mismanagement (of some £60,000 for which Ralegh claimed Sanderson never fully accounted), debt and forgery proceeded in Chancery and Star Chamber, but beneath the charges and counter-charges lay a dispute over credit and credibility, and protestations of toil....We have neither Chancery nor Star Chamber determinations in these cases – judgments may never have been handed down – but Sanderson appears to have been the abused party. Even Shelbury admitted that Sanderson 'was [so] careful and provident that he kepte continually five booke of Accompte the one for receipts and the other for disbursements everie daie setting down what was received and what disbursed and for what cause and by what warrantie...' Sanderson himself would insist on his 'painful endeavour' and 'great travell' on Ralegh's behalf, at one time or another standing bond with Ralegh, borrowing money at his own risk for Ralegh's use, even investing his own money, to the tune of £50,000 at one point, £30,000 at another" Professor Leinhard goes on to mention Sanderson's unsuccessful litigation with Sir John Watts (over the Bien Jesu), which resulted from Sanderson's efforts – on Ralegh's behalf – to relieve the Roanoke colony. Finally, he suggests that Ralegh eventually got his come-uppance, saying "While [Ralegh] may have set out on his first voyage to Guiana with a courtier's sense of satisfaction at having just trumped his merchant creditor, when he set sail on his second and final voyage to

Guiana it was King James, the creditor of final resort, who stacked the deck in his own favour. Matters were then arranged so that whether Ralegh succeeded or failed, James alone was guaranteed the advantage".

In 2002 Raleigh Trevelyan published his biography of Ralegh. He was clearly concerned about his subject's treatment of Sanderson, commenting (at p.567)"His behaviour towards Sanderson is worrying and not fully explained". He was also troubled about Harriot's direction in his will – that his old accounts with Ralegh should be destroyed – quoting (at p.564) Dr. Shirley's opinion that this represented " a very dark corner of Raleigh's and Harriot's association".

The ODNB was published in 2004. The article on Sanderson (by Dr Anita McConnell) describes his relationship with Ralegh, the Plymstock Incident in 1595, the litigation sixteen years later and the absence of any judgment or known outcome, and the fact that Sir William in An Answer was able to present his father in a better light than that painted by Ralegh's legal team. No opinion is offered on the "rights and wrongs" between the two men

Counting the Votes

We pass now to consider the eight opinions and judgments which have been offered on the legal and moral issues between Ralegh and Sanderson.

Only Professor Reinhard has raised his head above the parapet and he presents a powerful and clearly argued verdict against Ralegh. Rosalind Davies seems to have the same view, but her main interest is in Harriot's position. Raleigh Trevelyan is clearly uneasy about Ralegh's behaviour towards Sanderson. The other five avoid any conclusion or (what amounts to the same) find the scales exactly balanced.

Final Verdict.

No one denies Ralegh's abundant fine qualities – his personal bravery, wit, power of exposition, both verbal and written, presence and charm, but, equally, his contemporaries held him intolerably proud, ruthless, mendacious, selfish and an habitual "trouble-maker": in short, a great character with serious flaws. Sanderson, as we have attempted to demonstrate, was less gifted, less volatile and more rounded, and, as befits a successful merchant, steady, meticulous, loyal, at ease with those around him and patriotic in an unselfish way.

The contribution which each man brought to their relationship exactly reflects their respective characters. Thomas Harriot was, unwittingly, cast as the contemporary "umpire" or "referee" in the relationship between Ralegh and Sanderson. Remaining loyal to Ralegh throughout his life (despite becoming a "gentleman pensioner" of the Earl of Northumberland) he has been recognised, not only as one of the cleverest men of his generation, but also as devoid of worldly ambition and of complete integrity. Harriot knew Sanderson during the ten years or so during which they both served Ralegh. In 1595, on his master's instructions, he examined Sanderson's dealings on Ralegh's behalf during his treasurership and gave him a clean bill of health. His master accepted his conclusions, gave Sanderson a formal release – and then stole it back.

Ralegh did not financially ruin Sanderson but his actions obviously contributed to his ruin when his mining enterprise crashed. Payment by Ralegh (or his administrators) of only part of what he owed could, at any stage, have saved Sanderson from the moneylender and his other creditors and some eight or nine years in debtors' prisons.

No one has established that Sanderson ever damaged Ralegh or, indeed anyone else: the same cannot be said of Ralegh.[11]

On the material available, and with the contemporary evidence of Harriot as an expert witness, the moral high ground must undoubtedly be awarded to Sanderson. Ralegh's conduct at Plymstock was, at best, cynical and, at worst, calculating and wicked. .

On the litigation – if the two cases had proceeded to judgment – Sanderson would have won on all the issues.

APPENDIX A

Sir William's Biographical Notes on Sanderson

Sir William Sanderson

Sir William Sanderson's writings are the largest single biographical source for Sanderson and his family. Given the circumstances in which Sir William wrote them, it is important to consider whether we can safely rely on them.

Sir William was born c.1586. He was a courtier and monarchist. He suffered in the Civil War and was knighted by Charles II in 1660 when aged about 74 and served as a Gentleman of the Chamber. He was evidently a man of charm: on 9th May 1660, when seeking passage to visit the King at Breda he went to the fleet lying off Deal, and greeted Samuel

Pepys, apparently on first acquaintance, as "cousin" – to Pepys' amusement.[1] He married a baronet's daughter, Bridget Tyrrell She was often referred to as Dame Bridget and, later, was appointed "Mother of the Maids" by Catherine of Braganza, taking charge of the Queen's maids of honour. His writings were:-

(i) The Lives of Mary Queen of Scots and her son James (1656)
(ii) A Life of King Charles (1658)
(iii) Graphice (1658) a history of painting.
(iv) "An Answer" (1656)
(v) "Memoir by a Freind", found attached to "A Treatise of Exchange" published in 1626

(i) and (ii) were "monarchist" histories. They have not enjoyed a high reputation, being regarded as "partial and polemical"[2] We will deal later with (v) "Memoir by a Freind", which is usually attributed to Sir William. Sir William also became involved in the world of pamphleteering, written exchanges of views, often in violent (and therefore sometimes anonymous) terms on political, religious and other topics.

Sir William's first book (which we will refer to as "Lives of Mary and James") attracted a bitter anonymous attack by "A Lover of the Truth" in a pamphlet in the same year 1656 to which we will refer as "Observations" The author of "Observations" is usually identified as Carew Ralegh, Sir Walter's second son, though alternative attributions are (a) to the polemical divine Peter Helyn, probably writing with assistance from Carew Ralegh (b) some other person with the same assistance.[3] Carew Ralegh, like his mother Bess, was naturally sensitive about Ralegh's reputation and he certainly attacked another writer who queried whether Ralegh had any specific knowledge of a gold mine: the view that there was no identified gold mine was of course widely held at the time; and the Commissioners who examined Ralegh on his return to England reached the same conclusion. Modern historians take the same view, considering that, at most, Ralegh had hearsay reports about one or more mines. This conclusion is reinforced by detailed study of the differences between the published version of Ralegh's "Discoverie" and earlier MS versions which were circulated for comment, for example to Cecil. Comparison shows that the printed version was "spiced up", for the benefit of the Queen and potential investors, by emphasising the goldmining opportunities: see Discoverie p.xlvii ff. In 1595–6 Ralegh was trying to persuade the Queen to take an interest in Guiana and to appoint him as her imperial proconsul, and at the same time was trying to attract potential investors, so the exact location of goldmines was not a top priority: whereas when Ralegh pitched to James I some years later from the Tower an identified mine was essential to gain his release.

The "Observations" made a number of detailed criticisms of Sir William's book, including several affecting Ralegh which we will consider below. It is important to emphasise that, apart from the passages on Ralegh, there were many other criticisms quite unconnected with him, for example the treatment of the Earl of Essex (" a harsher censure....than any writer heretofore"); an "intimation" that the poisoning of Mary Queen of Scots was considered; that the treatment of James I was altogether too flattering; that William, Earl of Pembroke and Philip, Earl of Montgomerie "were men of considerable descents though of no fame in their merits"; that "he strives all he can to extenuate the foul murder" of Overbury; that he gave a "slight character" to Abbot, Archbishop of Canterbury; that he speaks "comtemptuously" of the Earls of Oxford and Essex "terming them young men, apprehending no danger, and so ignorant, they knew not how to avoid any"; that "all our marriages with Spain have been unfortunate to this Crown".

The "Lover of the Truth" criticised Sir William's treatment of Ralegh as follows:-

(i) While allowing him "a grand enemy to the Spaniard" he "believes him a conspirer with the Spaniard" (ii) At his trial at Winchester "He tired the Court and Jury with impertinences"(iii) "His voyage (to Guyana)....was a trick only to get his liberty and that he knew of no mine" (iv) "He sent out this voyage with other men's money" (v) Raleigh "had but a mean fortune which he meant to advantage by this voyage" (v) "They (the King's ministers and the Judges) had matter enough to take away his life in this his last business". Interleaved with these criticisms the author starts to fly his own kite, airing complaints about the treatment Ralegh received, for example, the composition of the jury at his trial; the failure to bring Cobham face to face with Raleigh; and recommending for a true account of the last Guyana voyage "Sir Walter Raleigh's own Apology now in print and to be had everywhere".

Because the bulk of the criticisms in "Observations" deal with people and matters other than Ralegh it would be wrong, as has sometimes been done, to describe the pamphlet war, of which it formed part, as being fought simply over Ralegh and Sanderson.

As seems to have been quite common in "pamphlet wars", the author of "Observations" seeks to bolster his criticisms of the "Lives of Mary and James" by launching scurrilous personal insults against Sir William as the author, his wife Dame Bridget and his father Sanderson senior: by to-day's standards this course appears unsavoury and indeed counter-productive. However, our interest is focussed on gaining information about the Sanderson family, and testing its evidential strength, so it is fair to comment that (i) the author of "Observations" is unlikely to have much of value to say about the Sandersons (ii) his apparent aim is to say unpleasant and wounding things about them, particularly Sir William as the author, in order to devalue the statements made in the "Lives of Mary and James" – so accuracy is unlikely to be high on his list of priorities. Again, since Sir William was no great historian, it may well be the case that the various criticisms are valid: but this is not relevant for present purposes.

We quote the main attack on Sanderson in full below for three reasons (i) since it is clearly at variance with Ralegh's allegations against Sanderson set out in the litigation between them, commenced in 1611 (ii) it underlines that the author was more interested in hurtful abuse than in accuracy (iii) it appears to be the source for criticisms of Sanderson, that he fell into arrears in accounting to Ralegh for income from the licences to import and retail wine, in two serious 19th century biographies, that of Ralegh by Edward Edwards, and of Harriot by Henry Stevens. "[Sanderson] was a gentleman, though poor,(but that I take to be no sin, though this man [i.e. Sir William] doth, and how he can clear himself from that offence, I know not) he was of kin to Siir Walter Raleigh, and in the time of his prosperitie and greatnesse was his servant, and intrusted with receiving great sums of money for him, out of his Office of Wines, and other his places, by which he came in arrears to Sir Walter Raleigh, in divers great sums: which after his troubles (being a prisoner in the Tower) Sir Walter sent unto Sanderson for; But he was so far from paying them (presuming that Raleigh was there friendlesse) that he pretended Sir Walter Raleigh should owe him £. 2000. Whereupon Sir Walter in great anger, commenced a suit against Sanderson which was managed by his servant and solicitor, John Shelbury, and Sanderson being overthrown and found in arrears to Sir Walter Raleigh, in very great sums, was cast into prison, and there died a poor contemptible beggar." James I cancelled Ralegh's right to licence the import and sale of wine in 1603. It was then debated whether arrears of fees due at that date should go to Ralegh as the office-holder at the time the fees accrued or to the new incumbent (Lord Nottingham). At that time it was some eight years since Sanderson had ceased to act as treasurer to Ralegh, so he could hardly have incurred any responsibility. If Sanderson had been withholding the Wine Office cash during his treasurership i.e in the ten years prior to 1595 this would have been picked up by Harriot when he audited Sanderson's accounts. As Sanderson was quick to point out in the litigation no criticism was ever made of his performance as treasurer while he was carrying out those duties. It is difficult to form a view as to whether the author of "Observations" muddled the "1603 arrears" with Sanderson's treasurership through misunderstanding or malice, but, in either case, the resulting statement was obviously damaging to Sanderson – so the versions of it that occur in Edwards and Stevens need to be re-considered. The other misstatements are:- (i) that the 1611 litigation was based on Wine Office arrears (In fact it was a claim for re-accounting for *all* pre-1595 transactions by Sanderson on Ralegh's behalf) (ii) that Sanderson was found "in arrears...in very great sums" to Ralegh (In fact no judgment was pronounced (iii) that Sanderson was, as a result, "cast into prison" (He was cast into prison but by a quite separate creditor) and "there died a poor contemptible beggar".(Not true)

Sir William lost no time in combating the insults and the criticisms of his historical efforts, and in the same year 1656 launched a riposte in his own name, which we refer to as "An Answer" Needless to say Sir William dealt in great detail with the "historical" points, but for present purposes we are more concerned with his treatment, again in great detail, of his own, his father's and his wife's backgrounds and lives. We have drawn on these throughout the book, at the same time noting both corroborative and conflicting evidence. Here we need to look at broader issues:- (i) Is Sir William telling the truth or is there some re-writing of history? (ii) Were Sir William's writings (in 1656) too long after the events related to carry much weight? (iii) What can we deduce about his attitude, and perhaps that of his siblings, towards their great uncle Ralegh? At least three of his brothers seem to have spent their lives "beyond the seas", and it is tempting to conclude that this may have happened because of the disgrace which fell upon their father, and the consequent shortage of funds.

Lapse of Time

Sir William 's "An Answer" in 1656 was written 18 years after the subject's death (1638) and over 100 years after his birth (c.1548). Sir William may have remembered important things as a little boy e.g. the Queen visiting the Sanderson home twice to accept the Molyneux globes, but any event prior to around 1595 is likely to be hearsay for Sir William. He definitely mentions that he was present on one or two occasions e.g. the Hounslow Heath meeting in 1603; visiting the Mines Royal operations. Other events are so graphically described e.g. the perpetual motion machine demonstration at the Islington house, that it seems that Sir William might have been present, even though he does not say so.

Sir William makes it fairly clear that as he writes he has Sanderson's cash books by him and also copies of the various treatises which Sanderson wrote on usury, foreign exchange, trade financing and so on. The cash books should, in principle, offset the hearsay handicap on financial matters but from the figures set out in the text of "An Answer" it looks as though Sir William did not understand too much of what he was reading.

A few "small" mistakes are found in Sir William's "An Answer"; none is material and they are such as may be expected after many years lapse of time; for example, the claim that the family's descent from Robert, Lord of Bedic in Durham *is included in the College of Heralds' pedigree;*[4] over the names of his father's ships which sailed with John Davis to the NW Passage and on the Roanoke voyages, and regarding the allocation of the spoils from the Madre de Dios in 1592, when he wrongly states that his father was a Commisioner and acted for the Queen. In general, however, much of his father's early history, as told by Sir William, can be corroborated from other sources: but when we come to "sensitive issues" Sir William seems to have "put the case" as favourably as possible to protect his father's memory.

Filial Bias – Stylistic Evidence

In general, the style of "An Answer" is an even-paced narrative, relaxed, with a good sprinkling of anecdote. However when sensitive subjects come up, for example Sanderson's financial or legal problems, or Ralegh or his wife, two changes are noticeable. The narrative becomes laconic, sometimes obscure; and, with the Raleghs, Sir William tends to lapse into sarcasm or open criticism. One can understand the hostility of Sir William (no doubt shared by his siblings) towards Ralegh following the insults and financial damage which his father suffered, and the resulting filial bias which tries to minimise or spin the financial problems which overwhelmed Sanderson; but it is clear that statements on these subjects must be treated with care. Some examples may be given

Best Friend to Money-Box ...

"But Sir Walter returning home to his Center the Court, his Sister's Daughter (Mrs Snedale) married to Sanderson,, who was become the Queens Customer and farmer, for the Over-lengths of Broad-cloaths; was pleased to descend so far, as to be a continuall guest at Sanderson's house, then in London, and Layton in Essex, and his best friend, it seems; whither he brought his Wife A Guest, himselfe then in disgrace concerning her, (I will be civill). And as Sir Walter's occasions had need, (Courtiers being not over-nice to make them often) he engaged Sanderson for him in £16,000 and was indebted besides to Sanderson in severall summes of money, as his Cash-books do yet evidence, amounting to £4000 (the Observator says, but £2000)". If Sir William's "spin" is removed it is clear that Sanderson became friendly with Ralegh and willingly became first "private banker" to his uncle-in-law and, subsequently, his general "man of business" or treasurer.

1611 Litigation

"And after Sir Walter's reprieve, became Suites in Law between Sanderson, about Sir Walter's debts, and Shelbury the solicitor: But, that Sanderson was then indebted, or ever arrested, or sued for debts of Arrears to him, or cast in Prison, or died in Prison, a poor contemptible beggar, is most untrue and scandalous". It suited Sir William to pass quickly over the 1611 litigation. Sanderson was indeed "cast into prison", but by his creditors, not by Ralegh, and stayed there from 1613 to 1622. Ralegh did not sue Sanderson "for debts of Arrears to him", but he did ask for full re-accounting for the period down to 1595 and claimed that the enormous sum of £60,000 had not been properly accounted for – so that, if the claim had been successfully pursued, some sums of money might have been due to Ralegh.

Conclusion

We may conclude, therefore, that we should not reject Sir William's account of his father's life and activities simply because of the lapse of time. As with any evidence we should check it carefully against other accounts, and – where the Sanderson/Raleigh quarrel is concerned – we should be particularly wary: it looks as though filial piety may have shaded his narrative.

Memoir by a Freind ("Memoir")

Much of the biographical material on Sanderson set out in "An Answer" is repeated in similar terms in "Memoir", which has come down to us attached to a paper on Usury produced in 1626. On some matters there is more detail (and there is one topic not mentioned at all in "An Answer"); and there are no references to the 1595 falling out between the two men.[5]

The Memoir is usually attributed to Sir William on the grounds (i) the content is similar to that of "An Answer" (ii) the paper on Usury – to which the Memoir was attached – was also written by Sir William. The second ground cannot now stand. In the past there has been some confusion between Sanderson and Sir William,[6] but it is now clear that Sir Wiliam was an "arts man" with no experience in commerce or finance and was quite unable to write on trade finance or "usury" (which at that period covered the lending of money between both merchants and private individuals, and was extremely complicated).[7] Sir William was clearly "in deep water" even when simply describing his father's skill in these subjects.[8] Further, he mentions that he had by him when writing "An Answer" a number of treatises by his father on trade financing subjects, as well as his cash books; while admiring his father's skills, he is clearly distancing himself from these complicated matters.

While ground (ii) thus cannot stand, the Memoir may still have been written by Sir Wlliam and there is a hint in the text of the Memoir to that effect. After describing the large sums raised by Sanderson for Ralegh (over £100,000 guaranteed and £16,000 borrowed on his own credit and made available to Ralegh) the writer continues "such was his Credit and Reputation in those days, *as there can be good proof thereof*". The phrase put into italics looks like a reference to the cash books of Sanderson which Sir William in "An Answer" claimed to have in front of him.

There is another possible item of evidence supporting Sir William's authorship of the Memoir. In listing the factual mistakes made by Sir William in An Answer we mentioned (see above p..) that he wrongly made Sanderson a Commissioner in the allocation of the spoils from the Madre de Dios carrack, when in fact he merely represented Ralegh and the officers and men serving. The Memoir seems to make the same mistake, stating "And hee was by the Qeenes Majestie special appointment put in Great Trust in the Business of both the Carrick's goods that came to London into Leaden hall both before and at his Majestie's coming to the Crowne of England"

Whether or not the work of Sir William, the Memoir duplicates the information in "An Answer" and thus, if written around 1626 (the date of the Usury paper to which it was attached), cuts down by some thirty years the lapse of time since the events referred to; and so corroborates what Sir William wrote in "An Answer".

Sir William in "An Answer" states that he has in his possession a number of papers written by his father on "the secret mysterie of Bullion and Monies, the exchange and rechange, single and double usance of Monies amongst Merchants; the Cambio Regis, of which the Treasurers, Burleigh and Sackville would say, That Sanderson understood the Theory and Practick more, than most English Merchants." Sanderson's main identified works on trade financing and economic matters are:-

(i)   Tract on Usury and a reply by Mr John Cotton (MS 1626)
(ii) "A Treatise of Echaunge, and of the Kinges Ma'esties Royal Exchaunger's Office" (MS 1626)
(iii) "A treatise of state merchant and of merchandising state, consisting of commerce, trade and traffique, and upheld by the King's Royal Exchangers Office" (MS 1629)

In addititon he contributed to reports issed by Commissions on these subjects, for example, he co-authored the 1622 Commission report with Sir Robert Cotton, Sir Ralph Middleon, John Williams and Gerard Malynes.

Sanderson seems to have developed something of a fixation on these subjects and to have bombarded James I and Charles I with "papers" on them right until the end of his long life.[9] Since his views remained constant over many years any effort to distinguish between originals, copies, summaries and so on would seem pointless.

APPENDIX B
Sanderson's Family & Pedigree

SANDERSON

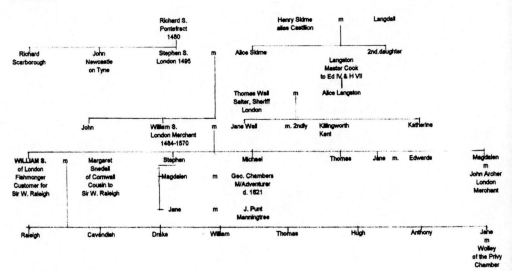

SOURCE: Vincent MSS, College of Heralds, 119 p.292

APPENDIX C
Thomas Allen's Imports

THOMAS ALLEN IMPORTS 1567–8

	Ship	From	Flax	cables	tar/pitch	poldavies	madder	value
9.10.67	Abraham	Danzig						£157
14.10.67	SeaWoolf	Amsterdam	5 packs	35 cwt				£63.8.4
31.10.67	Red Hart	Danzig	4 packs			30 pcs		£108.16.8
16.11.67	Nightingale	Danzig					45 cwt	£48
2.12.67	Bark Grey	Danzig						£48.3.4.
4.2.68	Thomas Allen	La Rochelle						£90
12.6.68	Jonas	Danzig	3 packs					£24
17.6.68	Daniell	Danzig						£76
15.6.68	Rose	Danzig	5 packs		30 lasts			?
28.2.68	Elizabeth	Danzig						£82.10.0.
25.6.68	Nightingale	Danzig	3 packs					£24
30.6.68	Bark Gray	Danzig						£143
7.7.68	Sampson	Hamburg						£60
10.7.68	George	Danzig						£24
14.7.68	Wildman	Danzig						£24
10.8.68	Mary Fortune	Danzig						£20
13.8.68	Whit Falcon	Amsterdam						£101

Total Value (11months) £791

Other goods imported in the same period included deals, wainscotts, clapholt i.e. clapboard, oar rasters, salt and iron.

APPENDIX D
"Honorary Treasurer" to Sir Walter Ralegh

In the ten years down to 1595 Sanderson assisted Ralegh in at least three ways (a) as treasurer (b) as banker, lending him money and guaranteeing his debts (c) providing advice on equipping ships and making available his own ships when needed e.g. to mount rescue efforts for the Roanoke settlement. It is therefore important to emphasise that Sanderson was much more than a skilful financial technician – his services to Ralegh were such as a partner might provide; though he was never remunerated and seems never to have profited from his work with Ralegh.

The Role of Treasurer

The overall responsibility of a treasurer or financial manager is to monitor and, as far as possible, to keep down the amount of cash employed in an enterprise. The routine way in which this is done is to maintain rolling forecasts of cash receipts and cash outgoings, and to "juggle" these, by accelerating receipts and postponing payments, so as to eliminate or to keep as small as possible the need for additional cash. If more cash is essential the treasurer is responsible for finding it, by equity investment or borrowing, and for negotiating the terms on which it is to be provided. If there are cash surpluses, he must turn them to best advantage by short-term investment or paying down debt. He must at all times keep au fait with the commercial ambitions of his principal – in order that the cash implications of new developments can be planned for: not an easy task with a man as mercurial and reckless as Raleigh.

Financial management in this sense is more commercial and entrepreneurial than routine book-keeping, but of course accurate recording of receipts and disbursements (and of the justifications for each transaction), and of funding arrangements is essential. In the 1611 litigation the Ralegh camp noticed, it would appear with some surprise, how meticulous Sanderson had always been in his recording of all cash transactions, both inwards and outwards, and of the need to record justification for each transaction.

Ralegh was lucky in having a very experienced and successful merchant like Sanderson performing this role for a number of reasons (1) He knew what was required and how to manage (2) As an independent merchant banker he was experienced in raising money (3) His own credit standing in London was high so that, where borrowing was needed, he could undertake it jointly and severally with Raleigh, who had no credit reputation, or borrow on his own. This was usually without collateral security, though following current practice under the usury laws[1] it was normal to have a "side deal" under which the borrower executed a recognisance, that is a formal undertaking registered with the court, to pay a higher sum (usually, it seems, about double the amount borrowed) if the original loan was not repaid by a specified date. See, for example, the loans to support the Roanoke Settlement from Thomas Smythe and John Watts, and Sanderson's own borrowing to finance the 1595 Manao/El Dorado expedition.

(4) When Sanderson lent his own money to Ralegh he seems not to have charged interest. This would have been in accord with his lifelong view that the old meaning of "usury" was correct – namely that a borrower should not be required to repay more than the original capital sum which he had borrowed.[2] Alternatively, Sanderson, as a wealthy man, may have simply felt that, just as he received no fee for working as Ralegh's "man of business", so he should not "make money out of" his uncle-in-law. (5) In addition to his financial skill, Sanderson knew a lot about organising freight, sea voyages and navigation from his experience as a merchant in North Europe, as patron and backer of John Davis and from his ownership of trading vessels. The Ralegh camp in the 1611 litigation belittled Sanderson's ship management experience – but this seems to be simply misrepresentation. (6) Sanderson provided his services for nothing. This point made him particularly bitter when he was betrayed by Ralegh in 1595.[3]

What did Sanderson actually do for Ralegh?

In the first two or three years, following their meeting as the result of Sanderson's marriage to Ralegh's niece, Sanderson acted as his private banker. He lent money to Ralegh and he acted as surety or guarantor when other parties provided goods or services to Ralegh on credit i.e. he undertook to pay if Ralegh did not. Sir William in An Answer has Ralegh requesting such assistance quite frequently, and states that "As Sir Walter's occasions had need … he engaged Sanderson for him in £16,000 and was indebted besides to Sanderson in several summes of money, as his Cashbooks do yet evidence, amounting to £4,000." Although Sir William was writing some 70 years later, it appears that he had Sanderson's cash books in front of him, and the amounts are in line with the extravagant spending for which Ralegh was renowned.

Sanderson's role soon enlarged in around 1585–6 and he appears to have become part of Ralegh's household, acting as treasurer or man of business, so that all Ralegh's cash transactions, both inward and outward, passed through his hands. He was formally appointed to represent Ralegh with regard to his rights, granted by the Queen, (i) to issue licences for the import and retailing of wine and (ii) to export overlengths of woollen cloth. This role was recognised when Sanderson was employed, in 1589, on government business (see p. above) and was officially described as "Ralegh's servant". Ralegh's representatives, in the 1611 litigation, when they were pressing for the Chancery Court to order re-accounting for transactions stretching back from 1595 for some 8–10 years, commented (with evident surprise) on the way in which he had carefully accounted for all inward and outward cash transactions, and urged that Sanderson should make available these detailed back records; thus demonstrating that everything done on Ralegh's behalf had been included in them. (Of course all these transactions had already been fully audited by Thomas Harriot in 1595, and, as a result, Ralegh had given Sanderson a full, unconditional release – something which, in 1611, Ralegh's representatives were seeking to downgrade to a "conditional release")

During this period, from around 1585 to 1595, Sanderson acted as Ralegh's treasurer in the full sense described above – handling all cash transactions and, in addition, where there were insufficient funds available, seeking additional money. This came from at least five sources (a) risk investment alongside Ralegh which would earn profit or suffer loss depending on their "share of adventure" i.e. their percentage of the total risk capital subscribed (b) risk investment in other forms. For example, in the Munster plantation Ralegh acquired seignories at his own expense and then "laid off" his expenditure and risk by selling leases to third parties. Again, in the reorganised second Roanoke settlement attempt in 1587 Ralegh formed an imposing Corporation of the Governor and Company of the City of Raleigh, in which he was careful to retain control, and sold shares in the corporation to third parties. Subscribers included Sanderson, along with Thomas Smythe (senior, the "Customer" i.e. farmer of the royal customs duties), Richard Hakluyt, Thomas Hood (the navigator) and many other merchants and gentlemen (c) loans from third parties, for example the loan of £1,500 from Customer Smythe in 1587 and the loan for £5,000 in 1590 from John Watts. Since no one would lend large sums to Ralegh without security, these loans were taken "jointly and severally" by Ralegh and Sanderson – which meant the lender could choose which of the borrowers he would look to for repayment – while such an arrangement held out Ralegh as one of the "principals" (d) loans by Sanderson of his own funds, probably (see above) free of interest. (e) loans by Sanderson of money which he had borrowed for the purpose from third parties on his own credit. Sanderson invested in this way for the Manao/El Dorado expedition in 1595 and Ralegh's failure to repay the investment in the region of £2,000 caused Sanderson to lose about £4000 because of the interest and penalties which he had to pay to his own lender.

Where additional funds were raised by loans it seems clear that Sanderson found the lenders, since Ralegh's credit was poor and it is hard to imagine him condescending to seek a loan and risk rejection. With risk investment, the picture was different, since such investment was made for personal and political reasons as well as for the hope of profit; and such investors included the Queen, Lord Burghley, and Sir Francis Walsingham. The risk investors who took leases of Ralegh's seignories in the Munster plantation were in a special category. They included some English landowners seeking to extend their estates (which was the original intention of the Plantation plan) but also some 18 merchants seeking to make money either from farming or from acquiring leases with a view to selling them on at a profit. Sanderson himself invested in Ireland – apparently as a speculation – buying the seignory of Castletown in 1592 from the original "undertaker" and selling it in 1602); so it seems reasonable to assume that Ralegh found the landowners and Sanderson the financial investors. Apart from the search for investors, it seems clear that Sanderson, with his knowledge of corporate finance, managed the financing operations.

Finally, we may note what may be called the "visibility problem". Many of Ralegh's projects, for example privateering expeditions, are described in surviving records without full details; in particular lacking any reference to Sanderson's involvement. If such projects fall within the 1586–1595 period – when Sanderson was acting as Ralegh's treasurer – we may nonetheless safely assume that the project's cash payments and receipts all passed through his hands and that the plan for financing the project was designed and managed by him. An important example is the Munster plantation, where we have already suggested (above p. 56) that, where there were insufficient English landowners to take up leases under Ralegh's seignories, Sanderson found City men prepared to invest, albeit with somewhat different objectives. No criticism seems to have been levelled at this strategy – which modified the original plan – just as Government accepted public servants and soldiers as "undertakers" when no more landowners came forward and tolerated the adoption of Irish tenants by the undertakers even though the original plan had specifically excluded them.

Ralegh Home & Colonial Enterprises
Cumulative Cashflow to 1595

The extent of Ralegh's financial resources, the cost of his lavish personal expenditure and the details of his financial collaboration with Sanderson are far from clear – and it is unlikely that they will ever be completely or accurately established – but it is suggested that a "guesstimated" cashflow will serve some useful purposes. First, it will give an indication of the scale on which Ralegh was operating, starting from a penniless arrival at Court in 1581. Secondly, it will permit, not conclusive, but credible answers to be given to some key questions, in particular, Did Ralegh fail to repay Sandersone the £4000 he owed him *because his funds were insufficient or because he chose not to do so?*. Was Ralegh's claim that Sanderson had failed to account adequately for some £60,000 of the funds which had passed through his hands realistic or fanciful?

Ralegh Home & Colonial Enterprises - Source & Disposition of Funds 1582-95

CASH AVAILABLE

	Value Est.	Annual Income Est.	Cumulative to 1595
1582 Entertainment allowance - Ireland	£100		
1582- Obtained Durham House			
1583 Two All Souls' lt (sold on)	£500		
Monopoly for importing/retailing wine		£1,500	£18,000
Monopoly for exporting undyed woollen broadcloths		£3,500	£42,000
1585* Lord Warden of the Stannaries		£2,500	£25,000
1587 Babington Estates		£1,000	£8,000
42,000 acres in Ireland		Nil	
1590 Bien Jesu prize	Nil		
1591 Privateering with Sir John Watts	£5,000		
1592 Madre de Dios prize	£2,000		
1592- Lease of Sherborne Estate		£1,000	
Other privateering	£5,000		
Totals to 1595	£12,600		£93,000

OVERALL CUMULATIVE 1582-1595   **£105,600**

*In 1585 Raleigh was also knighted and appointed Lord Lieutenant of Cornwall, Vice Admiral of the West, Governor of Portland Bill and joint Ranger of Gillingham Forest. In 1605 (9th.November) he wrote to the Privy Council stating that his income from the Governorship of Jersey (granted 1600), the Stannaries, Gillingham Forest and Portland Castle had exceeded £ 3.000

CASH DISPOSAL

	Amount Est.
Personal Expenditure (13 years @ £ 2,000 p.a.)	£26,000
1582 Durham House	£2,000
1583 Construction of Ark Royal	£4,000
1585 Roanoke settlement	£40,000
1592 Sherborne - Castle and Landscaping	£10,000
1594-5 Manoa/El Dorado - reconnaissance voyages	£4,000
main expedition	£30,000
Cumulative 1582-1595	£116,000

NOTES

1.With most figures guesstimated and a number of items omitted it is reasonable to assume that the total cash passing though Raleigh's and Sanderson's hands in the 1582-1595 period was between £ 100,000 and £ 150,000; perhaps £ 15-20 million in to-day's values.

2. Raleigh and Sanderson jointly borrowed £ 5,000 from Sir John Watts and £ 1,500 from Sir Thomas Smythe.(Since Raleigh's credit standing was poor, these loans were effectively on Sanderson's credit). These loans were repaid.

3. To finance the Manao/El Dorado expedition Sanderson borrowed on his own account. When the men quarrelled in 1595 Sanderson owed his lender £ 1,600 - 1,700 and it appears that Raleigh never reimbursed him.

4. The table of cash available (above) shows Raleigh's annual income, excluding "windfalls" e.g. from privateering, at £ 9,000. It seems reasonable to assume that he continued to receive around £ 10,000 p.a. until his downfall on the accession of James I.

APPENDIX E
Lending and Usury[1]

Moneylending contracts during the period 1550–1625 were governed by a number of statutes, not by judge-made law, so they reflected the views of the legislators and those to whose opinions they listened, including statesmen, divines, merchants and lawyers. The main statutes were passed in 1545 (Henry VIII), 1552 (Edward VI), 1571 (Elizabeth) and 1624 (James I).

At every stage the debate centred on the meaning of "usury", which to-day we regard as "lending on extortionate terms", but which in the mid-16th century meant the lending of money under a contract which gave to the lender **any financial benefit over and above the return of the capital sum lent.** This was based on a number of extracts from the Old and New Testaments and the opinions of the Early Fathers i.e. religious or ethical standards, to which, it was felt, the laws of the land must conform. There were a few exceptions which were considered to escape divine condemnation, for example the Monarch might borrow at interest to support the public finances; dependent persons, like widows or orphans, might lend, or have loans arranged for them, at interest out of their capital in order to support themselves; and officially organised lending or pawnbroking institutions might advance money to the poor. This strict view effectively ignored the widespread practice of lending and borrowing which took place in all parts of English society whether commercial, for example, farmers, manufacturers and shopkeepers who needed finance to tide them over until their efforts generated a cash income, or purely domestic within families or between neighbours. It is clear, too, from the reported cases, that there were professional moneylenders, not necessarily full-time, both in towns and in the country. In the second half of the 16th century, with commerce operating on a larger scale and English merchants moving into international business, the need for commercial credit expanded but the religious purists continued to argue vehemently against any relaxation. The tide eventually began to turn around 1600 when the religious based view which had up till then prevailed was overtaken by the secular approach which, while recognising the evils of extortion, maintained that the law should be divorced from religious or moral considerations and reasonable rates of interest should be permitted in the interests of commerce and prosperity.

The ebb and flow of opinion was reflected in the statutes listed above. The 1545 Statute, unlike its predecessors, did not quote divine authority as the basis for controlling "usury". It permitted lending with interest at up to 10% but provided that on loans with a higher rate the lender could be called upon to pay a penalty of three times the capital sum. Enforcement, as under the earlier statutes, was delegated to informers, who would receive half the penalty, with the balance going to the Crown. In practice informers tended to threaten lenders and compound with them for a smaller amount. It seems that this Act was ineffective to prevent loans at higher rates of interest and the "religious lobby" in 1552 passed a new statute which repealed the 1545 Act, reintroduced divine authority as the basis and totally prohibited lending at interest. The penalty for a lender was the sum of the principal and the interest. Not surprisingly this tightening of the law failed to stem loans at high rates of interest and a number of schemes were developed to evade the prohibition by concealing or disguising the true transaction. From 1545 to 1552 the interest in excess of 10% needed to be concealed; from 1552 to 1571 all the interest, and after 1571 the interest over 10%: at least 12 different categories of artificial transactions were designed for these purposes.[2] The volume of the lending transactions is illustrated by the increase in the number of actions by informers.

In 1563 there was an unsuccessful attempt to repeal the 1552 Act. In 1571 after extensive debate a new attempt was made to improve the situation. The 1571 Statute revived the 1545 Act but stiffened its terms, thus effecting a compromise between the 1545 and 1552 Statutes. Divine authority prohibiting usury was re-introduced and all loans at interest were prohibited, except those to support orphans. The prohibition included loans with interest up to 10% but since the penalty in this class of case was much lower (the amount of the interest only) it was not worthwhile for informers to attack them; so in practice such loans became tolerated. Where interest exceeded 10% the contract itself was declared void, the penalty was three times the capital sum and, in addition, brokers who arranged such loans could now be penalised.

After 1600 there were a number of attempts made in Parliament to strengthen the regulation of "usury" but these were mainly directed to reducing interest rates on economic grounds, for example, because high interest rates depressed trade and because it was thought that the returns from moneylending were so attractive that they discouraged men from active commerce. Religious arguments continued to decline and by the debate on the 1624 Statute had virtually disappeared. That Act reduced the acceptable interest rate level to 8% and imposed limits on (i) the fees charged by brokers for organising loans and (ii) the charges for drawing up the bonds by which loans were secured; these two upfront items, which had provided scope for fleecing borrowers, were subject to an overall cap of 0.3% of the loan.

APPENDIX F
Ralegh's Letter to the Master of the Rolls

Letter from Ralegh to the Master of the Rolls

(Reproduced from Yoiungs pp.320–321)

Dated 19th June 1611

To my honorable frinde Sir Edward Phillips' knight, Master
of the Rolls

Having herd that the commission sent into Devon is returned, I beseich
yow to give us some end of the unchristian sute which Sanderson hath
agaynst me. Before the commission was sent it was proved by Mr Heriots
oath that my release to Sanderson was but conditionale, yea, his owne
borrowing of it for certayne dayes to shew his creditors, and his restoring of
it to Heriot agayne, did sufficiently prove it. For the bond of myne for a
braslett of seed perrell, I trust, Sir, that yow will not thinck it reasonable
that I pay that bond before he deliver up bonds of myne for twenty or
thirtye thowsand pound which, I am told, he hath gotten assigned over to
him self. I was ever contented to allow him that bond uppon his accompt,
though it be 200li for 20li, but if he be ten thowsand pound in my debt I
trust that yow will not charge me to pay him who hath little or no meanes
to pay mee. For a paper which I sheweth of myne, noated in the margerxt
by my self, I beseich yow, Sir, to understand it aright, which is that I never
signed to any thing therin but to myne owne margent to the end to give
allowance to pass in his acccompt such somes agaynst which I did not
accept. For he told me that he had no warrant for them and that therfore
my auditor would not allow them, which perswaded mee to the signing of

- 155 -

that paper in the margent, not that I ever acknowleged any of those summs payd by him otherwise than with my mony.

And, Sir, wheras he made but a slight matter of the careck accompt, I will shew it yow if yow please that he received of the carrek goods six and thirty thowsand pound, which, with the two and forty thowsand which he chargeth him self withall, amounteth to seventy eyght thowsand pound.

Lastly, Sir, this pernitious miscreant bath vaunted to one of the custome howse to whom he is indebted, that he was promised a judgment of 500li agaynst mee in the Roles before the matter was herd, and he that will dare to abuse a man of yowr venue and reputation in the world will easely scandale a man in adversitie and frindles.

But for my self, as it was never in my power to do yow service, so have I ever loved and honored yow and will rest reddy to be commanded by yow.

June the 19

W Ralegh

APPENDIX G
Gwyana / Guyana – Use as a place name

1. Report from the National Maritime Museum

——-Original Message——-
From: MICHAEL FRANKS [mailto:michaelfranks68@btinternet.com]
Sent: 23 November 2005 18:14
To: Brian Thynne
Subject: William Sanderson (c.1548 – 1638)Guyana – Gwyana – Guiana

Bryan Thynne Esq
Curator of Hydrography
NMM

Dear Mr. Thynne,

You may remember providing me with some very useful information on the globes of Emmerie Molyneux about this time last year. I am now worrying at another William Sanderson problem on which I would welcome your views. The point is cartographical but it arises, somewhat unexpectedly, as an issue in the vicious litigation in which Sanderson was involved with Raleigh.

After a short successful career as a North Europe merchant, Sanderson returned to London c.1578 and in 1584 married a niece of Sir Walter Raleigh and became friendly with him. From around 1584 until 1595 he served as Raleigh's man of business or "Honorary Treasurer" (an apt description, since Raleigh never rewarded him).

In 1595 Raleigh was planning his expedition to find Manao or El Dorado in South America, having obtained the Queen's permission to leave England to command it. Sanderson accordingly sought a general settlement of accounts for his treasurership (in case Raleigh failed to return) and formal releases were exchanged.(The general settlement established that Raleigh owed Sanderson around £2,000 the bulk of which Sanderson had borrowed from a third party on his own sole credit) On the eve of his departure Raleigh tricked Sanderson into handing back the release document which he had given him (and all the supporting material) – which he then passed to his servant, the polymath Thomas Harriot, saying that if he (Raleigh) died on the expedition the release would stand, but if he returned, Sanderson would have to re-account for all the transactions prior to 1595. Sanderson protested, lost his temper and walked out. The two never worked together again, but the two families – the Sandersons and the Raleighs – appear to have remained on friendly terms.

Raleigh never repaid Sanderson what he owed him, and it appears that, with interest and penalties, the debt increased to around £4,000. In 1610 or 1611 Sanderson formally demanded repayment from the "administrators" appointed to manage Raleigh's assets and to pay his debts (following his attainder for treason). On Raleigh's instructions the administrators refused and commenced Chancery proceedings against Sanderson, demanding a re-accounting for all the transactions on Raleigh's behalf in the years prior to 1595. By any standards the claim was extraordinarily weak and "stale". Sanderson resisted the claim and counterclaimed. When the formal release (granted by Raleigh to Sanderson in 1595) was eventually produced in Court it was found to have on it an "endorsement", signed by Sanderson, Raleigh and witnesses stating (as Raleigh had unilaterally maintained in 1595) that the release was "conditional" not absolute; so that, as Raleigh had returned safely from South America, Sanderson was due to render a fresh account of all the transaction 15+ years before. Sanderson protested that the endorsement was a forgery and when the Chancery Court failed to investigate this claim effectively, commenced separate proceedings in Star Chamber offering detailed evidence of how the forgery had been carried out. To demonstrate that it was forged he also relied on the fact that the endorsement referred to Raleigh's 1595 expedition as being to Gwyana – stating that this place name had never been used in England until Raleigh himself used it on his return.

Sanderson owned ships and was familiar with charts and navigation (John Davis attested to this), and he had assisted Raleigh with the operational preparations for the 1595 expedition, as well as raising the necessary funds, and would hardly have made this very specific allegation to Star Chamber unless he was sure of his ground. The only scholar who seems to have considered the matter[1] discounted this allegation by Sanderson but then went on to say that he had not found any reference to Guyana prior to

Raleigh's own charts published on his return. I suppose that any earlier writings or charts are likely to have been Spanish, or perhaps French or Dutch, rather than English. Even if one or more of these is found to feature Gwyana or Guyana or Guiana this does not necessarily conclude the matter, for Sanderson was simply saying that the name was not in use in England in January/February 1595 when the endorsement purported to have been drafted. If no recorded mention at all of Gwyana or Guyana or Guiana is found prior to that time Sanderson's case on the point is obviously strengthened.

I have located one earlier chart or map of the area in the listing on your website (I think Dutch), but I have not viewed it[2] and no doubt there are more in the BL and other collections.

The name Guyana is usually derived from Amerindian words – the most popular version being "land of many rivers" – but the initial "g" may have been added by the Spanish.

I would be most interested to hear if you can cast any light on this question.

Best Wishes
Michael Franks

Dear Mr. Franks.

Thank you for your e-mail message of the 23 November 2005. Please do accept my apologies for the delay in responding to your enquiry. A period of annual leave and pressing work commitments on my return to the office have prevented a reply sooner.

I read with interest your description of the account of the disagreement between the merchant William Sanderson and Sir Walter Ralegh over the expenses associated with the latters first voyage to Guiana in 1595.

Although familiar with Sanderson's financial involvement and support of Ralegh's expeditions to the New World, I must confess that I have not made a detailed study of the circumstances and conclusion of the matter' that eventually ended up being settled in Star Chamber.

After the discovery of Guiana in 1498, I believe that the coastline was first charted by the Spanish in about 1499. Certainly the coastline was mapped by the following century, and the area is covered in some detail on a large scale Portuguese manuscript chart, which is contained in an atlas of about 1550–60 (Ref.P14–12v) which is kept in our museum collections. Although Guiana is featured by the anonymous cartographer, the region is not named Guiana, Guyana or Gwana on the chart. Examination of contemporary material from our holdings by Reinel (Portugese) c.1535;

Freducci (Italian) 1555; Deslien's 1567 and Hamon 1568 (both French); Martines 1572 (Italian) and of course the maps of America by Ortelius (1570) and Mercator (1595), also, do not produce any evidence of the name being used at that time.

Perhaps the most interesting factor is my consultation of the atlas produced by the geographer Cornelis van Wytfliet (d.1597), titled 'Descriptionis Ptolemaicae augmentum', which was first published in 1597, with another edition appearing later that year and a further issue a year later in 1598 (we have copies of the books for both 1597 and 1598 in our collections). Wytfliet's work consists of a historical narration of the discovery of the New World, its geography and natural history. The atlas is recognised as one of the most important developments in the research of the history of the New World. The volume is exclusively concerned with the American regions. One of the 19 regional maps included in the compilation is 'Residuum continentis cum adiacentibus insulis', which concentrates on the coast of Guiana and the Caribbean. On no part of this map can the name Guiana, Guyana or Gwana be observed. Considering the relevance of this atlas, I believe that if this name for the region, was in general use in Europe (and England) at the time, then the fact would be recorded on this map and in the accompanying text. To add support to this theory, the Boazio maps of 1589, depicting Drake's West Indian Voyage to the West Indies in 1585–6 also do not mention Guiana in the cartography. It seems probable that the name Guiana, Guyana, or Gwana does not appear on maps and charts until the early 17th century, with for example, Ralegh's own map of the area, and the publications after Ralegh's first expedition by Hondius and De Bry. I can only arrive at this verdict after consulting the relevant available maps, charts and records held here at Greenwich. There is always a possibilty that another establishment may have in its archives an earlier example of the name Guiana, Guyana or Gwana being used on productions or publications of the area under discussion, however from my own findings here at the NMM , I am inclined to side with Sanderson's view in his dispute with Ralegh, that the place name had never been used in England (or maybe even in Europe), before Ralegh's return from the first 'El Dorado' voyage.

I do hope that my provided information and views prove to be of interest.

Yours sincerely
Brian Thynne
Curator of Hydrography

2. Report from the British Library

11th June 2007

Dear Mr Armitage,

Further to our conversation on Thursday, apologies for not following up sooner, but I have only got back to my desk this morning.

The cartographical question arises from a disputed document. An endorsement on a deed referred to Ralegh's intended trip to Gwyana. The parties holding the deed maintained that the endorsement had been added prior to 6th February 1595 when Ralegh sailed from Plymouth for South America. The parties challenging the authenticity of the endorsement maintained that the endorsement could only have been added after Ralegh's return, around September 1595, **because Ralegh personally brought back the name "Gwyana" &c. and introduced it to England.** Prior to departure the expedition had been described as being to Manao or El Dorado.

The National Maritime Museum looked at the question in 2003 – I left you copies of our exchange of messages. The NMM were careful to say that they had not searched beyond their own collections. It occurred to me that you might have charts &c which the NMM does not, in which case it would be interesting to see whether they tell the same story. Any other observations which you might have on the question would be most welcome too.

Kind Regards
Michael Franks.

From: <u>Armitage, Geoff</u>
To: <u>MICHAEL FRANKS</u>
Sent: Friday, June 22, 2007 3:28 PM
Subject: RE: Gwyana/Guyana/Guiana – first use in England as placename

Dear Michael

Somewhat surprisingly I have located a manuscript Spanish map of the Orinoco and Amazon area dated about 1560 in Archivo Historico Nacional, Madrid which seems to show the name Guayana. It is illustrated in R A Skelton *Explorers maps* (1958) on page 88. The name is in lower case and not very conspicuous. I only spotted it with a magnifying glass. You would be very welcome to come in and verify this.

Sincerely
Geoff Armitage

26 June 2007

Dear Geoff,

Many thanks for your message and apologies for not replying sooner – I have been away for a couple of days.

Finding "Gwyana" (or similar) on any pre-1595 chart might prima facie seem to challenge the conclusion which appears to be emerging – that this place name was not known in England at the relevant time. However, your find in fact seems to me to confirm the conclusion (as above) – since the chart in question is MS and not well-known. The party alleging forgery of the endorsement did not say that Ralegh had made up the name – clearly it was in use in South America and (as your MS chart illustrates) known to Spaniards; simply that it was not in use in England until introduced by Ralegh personally. So it still looks as though the "dodgy" lawyer who drafted the endorsement unintentionally indicated that it was drafted after Ralegh's return, not, as they were maintaining, before he left.

I don't think that I mentioned previously that in the text of the endorsement itself there is considerable internal evidence suggesting forgery, including the omission of a date – always standard practice where formal legal rights are involved.

Thank you very much for taking so much trouble. Sadly I won't be into the BL for a bit but will, if I may, give you a shout ahead of my next visit and hope to see the map then.

Kind Regards – and many thanks
Michael

Abbreviations & Sources

1421	1421 The Year China discovered America, Gavin Menzies. Bantam 2002
After Elizabeth	After Elizabeth, Leanda de Lisle. Harper Perennial 2006
An Answer	An Answer to a Scurrilous Pamphlet intituled "Observations"[q.v.]
APC	Acts of the Privy Council
Aubrey	Brief Lives, John Aubrey. Penguin 1978
BL	British Library
Bawlfe	The Secret Voyage of Sir Francis Drake, Samuel Bawlfe. Penguin 2003
BEB	Extinct Baronetage, Burke
Bess	Bess, Anna Beer. Constable 2004
Brief and True Report	A Brief and true report of the new found land of Virginia, Thomas Harriot. 1588
Canny	Making Ireland British 1580–1650, Nicholas P. Canny. OUP 2001
CSP	Calendar of State Papers
	Certain Errors of Navigation, Edward Wright 1599
Champion Article	Religion in Tudor Shrewsbury, W. A. Champion 2006
	Commission for Sale of Prizes taken by Sir Walter Raleigh's Fleet", dated 30th October 1592
Cotton	An Elizabethan Guild of the City of Exeter, William Cotton 1873
Craster Article	Elizabethan Globes at Oxford, Sir Edmund Craster. The Geograhical Journal (March 1951) 117:1:24–6

Creature in the Map	The Creature in the Map, A Jorney to El Dorado, Charles Nicholl. U of Chicago Press 1995
Crino/Wallis article	Der Globusfreund 35–7 (1987) 11–18 "New Researches on the Molyneux Globes", A.N.Crino & H.M.Wallis
DNB	Dictionary of National Biography
Davies Paper	"Thomas Harriot and the Guiana Voyage in 1595", Rosalind Davies, Durham Thomas Harriot Seminar, Occasional Paper No.24, 1997
Derbyshire Lead Industry	Derbyshire Lead Industry in the 16th century. D.T. Kiernan. Chesterfield: Derbyshire Record Society 14. 1989
Description and Use of the Sphere	Description and Use of the Sphere, Edward Wright 1613
Discourse to the Queen	Discourse to the Queen, Humphrey Gilbert 1576
Discoverie	The Discoverie of the Large Rich and Bewtiful Empire of Guiana, Ralegh 1596. (ed. Joyce Lorimer) The Hakluyt Society 2006
Donald	Elizabethan Monopolies, M.B.Donald. Oliver & Boyd 1961
Dorset Elizabethans	Dorset Elizabethans, Rachel Lloyd. John Murray 1967
Drake	Sir Francis Drake and the Famous Voyage 1577–80 (ed. Norman Thrower) U of California Press 1984
EHMC	The Early History of the Muscovy Company, T.S.Willan. Manchester UP 1956
EL	Elizabeth's London, Liza Picard. Weidenfeld & Nicholson 2003
EPV	English Privateering Voyages, Andrews, K.R. Hakluyt Society 1959
Elizabeth	Big Chief Elizabeth, Giles Milton. Sceptre 2000
Forman	Dr Simon Forman, Judith Cook. Vintage 2002
Frobisher	Martin Frobisher, James McDermott.Yale UP 2001
God and the Moneylenders	God and the Moneylenders, Norman Jones. Basil Blackwell 1989
HV	Principal Navigations of the English Nation, Richard Hakluyt.
HFC	Hampshire Field Club, Proceedings of
HL	House of Lords

Harben	A Dictionry of London, Harben. 1918
Harriot	Life of Thomas Harriot, Dr John Shirley. Oxford 1983
Hues	Tractatus de Globis, Robert Hues. 1594
Instructions	Instructions to His Son and to Posterity, Ralegh. 1632
Leyton Register	Leyton Register, Vestry House Museum, Walthamstow
Limitation	Limitation of Actions, Michael Franks. Sweet & Maxwell, 1959
Markham	Voyages of John Davis, Sir Clements Markham. Hakluyt Society LIX 1880
McIntyre Article	William & Mary Quarterly 1956 Vol. xiii. 184, Dr Ruth McIntyre
Memoir	Memoir by a Freind c.1626
Mercator	Mercator, Nicholas Crane, Phoenix. 2003
Munster Plantation	The Munster Plantation 1583–1641, Michael McCarthy-Murrogh. Univ of London 1983
Muscovy Merchants	The Muscovy Merchants of 1555, T.S.Willan. Manchester UP 1953
Natural History of Wiltshire	John Aubrey MS c.1690.
Observations	Observations upon Some particular Persons and Passages in a Book lately made publick intituled A Compleat History of the Lives and Reignes of MARY Queen of Scotland and of Her Son James The sixth of Scotland and the First of England France and Ireland
ODNB	Oxford Dictionary of Nationaal Biography, OUP. 2004
Pepys	Diary, Samuel Pepys
Prince Henry	Henry, Prince of Wales, Roy Strong. Thomas & Hudson 1986
RGS	Royal Geographical Society
RV	Roanoke Voyages, David Quinn.Hakluyt Society CIV 1955
Raleigh	Sir Walter Raleigh, Raleigh Trevelyan. Penguin 2002
Ralegh & Marlowe	Ralegh & Marlowe, E.G.Clark. Fordham U Press, NY 1941
SPD	State Papers (Domestic)
SP Foreign	State Papers Foreign

Salisbury MS	Calendar of MSS preserved at Hatfield House, HMSO
	The Seaman's Secrets, John Davis. 1594
Shirley Article	Huntington Library Quarterly 1949–50, XIII 55–69, Dr John Shirley
	Sir Walter Raleigh, Edward Edwards 1865
Sir William	Sir William Sanderson
STAC	Star Chamber
Stowe	The Survey of London, John Stowe (ed. C.L.Kingsford) OUP 1908
Subsidy Roll	City of London Subsidy Rolls 1541/1582 (ed. R.G.Lang) London Record Society 1992
Supple	Commercial Crisis and Change in England 1600–42, B.E.Supple. CUP 1959
	The Surveyor's Dialogue, John Norden. 1607
	Tractatus de Globis, Robert Hues. 1594
	Traverse Book, John Davis. 1587
	Thomas Harriot, Henry Stevens, London 1900.
Use of the Globes	The Use of both the Globes, Celestiall and Terrestriall, most plainely delivered in the form of a Dialogue, Thomas Hood, 1592
WHD	The Worlde's Hydrological Description, John Davis.1594 (reprinted in Markham)
Wallis 1951 Article	The Geographical Journal 1951 "The First English Globe: a recent discovery", Helen Wallis.
Wallis 1955 Article	The Geographical Journal 1955 CXXI 3, 304 "Further light on the Molyneux Globes", Helen Wallis.
Wallis 1989 Article	"Opera Mundi" Emery Molyneux, Jodocus Hondius and the first English globes, Helen Wallis, Theatrum Orbis Librorum: Liber Amicorum 1989
	Sir Walter Raleigh, Edward Edwards, London 1900
Youings	The Letters of Sir Walter Raleigh (edd. Agnes Latham, Joyce Youings) Univ. of Exeter 1999

Picture Credits

Ownership and permission to reproduce are gratefully acknowledged.

Front Cover: "A Procession of Queen Elizabeth" by Peake the elder. Sherborne Castle.
Back Cover (1) Watercolour "Sherborne Lodge" (Ralegh's mansion c. 1600) (2) Photograph of Sherborne Castle to-day. Both at Sherborne Castle.

p.viii Durham House. Engraving; p xii Traditional portrait (though now doubted) of Thomas Harriot The President and Fellows, Trinity College, Oxford; p.13 Gerardis Mercator and Jodocus Hondius. Coloured engraving; p.38 Dr John Dee Engraving; p.39 Chart "The North West Passage Explorations of John Davis" The Hakliyt Socirty; p.48 Engraving "Roasnoke" De Bry 1590; p.53 19th century map showing area of Ralegh's Munster seignories'; p.55 Engraving "Myrtle Grove"; p.58 Terrestrial and Celestial Globes. The Honourable Society of the Middle Temple; p,65 The arms of William Sanderson, enhanced by order of the Queen; The Royal Geographical Society; p.75 Photograph of the fire-place in Ralegh's study at Shertorne Castle. Sherborne Castle; p.75 Engraving of the king or chief being coated with gold dust, De Bry 1590; p.77 Modelled in gold, a balsa raft The Gold Museum, Bogota; p.78 Sketch of Ralegh's map of Orinoco/Amazon area; p.97 The arms of the Mines Royal and of the Mineral and Battery Works Companies; Appendix A. Engraving of Sir William Sanderson.

Notes

Introduction

1   An interesting account of James' assumption of power is given in *After Elizabeth*.

2   SPD iv 76.

3   This account was written, many years later in 1656, by William Sanderson, junior, in a biographical note on his father's life, which appeared in a pamphlet to which we refer, in abbreviation, as "An Answer": see further below p. ff. and Appendix A.

4   The functions of a "treasurer" or financial manager, and the duties actually performed by Sanderson for Ralegh in that role, are considered in Appendix D.

5   See Youings p.321.

6   See p.73.

7   Bess's biographer, however, has Bess giving instructions to Ralegh's administrators to commence proceedings against Sanderson in 1611, suggesting that Bess had "turned against" the Sandersons: see Bess p.191.

8   See Harriot.

9   See Harriot p.348.

10 See McIntyre Article.

11 See Shirley Article.

12 See below p.129.

13 Raleigh p.567.

Part One – Worshipful Citizen and Fishmonger

1   For the full title see Abbreviations at p.63ff.

2   Ibid.

3   See Appendix A.

4   Sanderson's petition to the Star Chamber in 1613 is valuable in explaining how he met and became close to Raleigh.
5   See Appendix B]

Chapter 1 – A Younger Son

1   For example John Sanderson, the well-known Levant merchant (1560–1611) and Robert Sanderson, Bishop of Lincoln, (1587–1663).
2   See An Answer, "My Father...whose extraction and descent antiently from Robter("Robert"), Lords of Bedic in the Bishoprick of Durham , as is appears by his Pedigree enrowled in the Office of Arms".
3   See pedigree in Appendix B.
4   See Appendix B.
5   See Herbert, Fishmongers' Company p.7.
6   There were two halls when fishmongers were divided into stockfishmongers and saltfishmongers, but when they combined in 1535 only one was preserved, fronting the River Thames just off Thames Street.
7   At that time Billingsgate Market was handling the import by water of all kinds of food and only specialised later in fish: see Stowe p.206; E.L. p.150.
8   See the pedigree in Appendix B: Killingworth may have been the man of that name who was a factor, at some time the chief factor, of the Muscovy or Russia Company resident in that country.
9   The location is further discussed below at p.1.
10 As a result literacy levels in London were high, being around 70% by 1600.

Chapter 2 – Merchant Beyond the Seas

1   This is one possibility – and apprenticeship was by far the commonest method of joining a City company: the other is that he became a Fishmonger by redemption on returning to London in 1578 when aged about 30.
2   For further details on his life and trading activities – for example he operated a rope walk at Greenwich – see Muscovy Merchants p. 75.
3   See CSP Domestic 1581–90, where in July 1581 there is a note of "flax, hemp, tallow and other stores shipped at the Narve in Sweden on account of Mr. Thomas Allen, for the Queen Majestie's use"; and Appendix C, where details and values of Allen's imports over ten months in 1576–7 are listed.
4   Extensive information on this trade, and how it was conducted, has been preserved in the early records of the Muscovy Company, formed in 1555: see EHMC.

5   Michelmore returned later to plague the EIC as the first "interloper", authorised by James I to trade in the East Indies despite the monopoly granted in 1600 to the Company by Queen Elizabeth.

Chapter 3 – Merchant to Merchant Banker

1   Sanderson proved the will of his elder brother Stephen on 15th October 1577.

2   The holding was at Castletown, Limerick and extended to some 3274 acres. The writer who describes the Plantation doubts whether Sanderson ever went there; since many wealthy English bought as investors with no intention of settling: see Munster Plantation p.124.

3   See Leyton Register.

4   See Harben "Hoop Yard, Tavern": this part of Thames Street was also referred to by its older name of Stockfishmongers Row.

5   He dined at the Hoop on Fish Street Hill on 21st September and 9th November 1660 and at the Hoop in Thames Street on 10th January 1661.

6   In 1613 Sanderson mortgaged a house/inn in Lower Thames Street called the Golden Hoop to his moneylender George Pit: see p.116 below. It looks as though the explanation is that the Sanderson family had owned several adjoining buildings in Thames Street, see p.117.

7   Although An Answer describes him as a Royal Navy commander, and the Heralds' pedigree says the Snedalls were from Cornwall: see Appendix B.

8   "In the continuance of time and by reason principally of my insight in this study (i.e. geography and cartography) I grew familiarly acquainted with the chiefest Captaines at sea, the greatest Merchants, and the best Mariners of our nation": see the Dedication, addressed to Sir Francis Walsingham, of the first edition of The Principle Navigations, published in 1589.

9   Described below p.58ff.

Chapter 4 – A Link with Frobisher?

1   Sanderson did not figure in the original DNB.

2   Sanderson as executor proved the will of his elder brother Stephen on 17th October 1577.

3   Lane's report is in HV III 330ff.

4   See Frobisher, passim.

5   See Frobisher, published in 2001 and the article by the same author in ODNB 2004.

Chapter 5 – Other Interests for a City Man

1   See above p.6.

2   Ibid.

3   See below p.29.

4   See above p.6.

5   See ODNB article om Burghley, "The management of the economy".

6   Apart from patriotism the choice of overseas careers by the younger sons may also have been influenced by their father's financial "crash" in the first decade of the 17th. century, resulting in the collapse of his City reputation and the family's shortage of ready money.

7   See above p.6.

8   See below p.85ff.

9   See further below p.97.

10 Ralegh's only ship command seems to have been the Falcon in the unsuccessful voyage in 1578–9 led by Humphrey Gilbert.

11 He may also be the same John Chilton who made a 17 year journey through the Spanish Empire in Central America, which is recorded in HV Vol. IX. 360ff.

12 See Appendix B.

13 See EPV p.41. Sanderson was to borrow £5,000 from Watts in 1590, probably to finance the Roanoke settlements, and was to be defeated by him in the Admiralty Court, though it is thought that there may have been a compromise deal behind the scenes, over the prize money on the Buen Jesus in 1591: see below p.50.

14 See List & Analysis of SPForeign 1589–90 para 751; Ibid. 1590–1 para 798

15 See Salisbury MSS Pt IV p.239 and, for a fuller description, p.73 below.

16 Gerald Malynes was not, of course. an assistant of Sanderson's, but a fellow economist who shared "mercantilist" views.

17 Considered in more detail at p.21ff.

18 The Devon weaving industry imported Merino wool via Barnstaple.

19 See, for example, the comment of John Aubrey, himself a sheep farmer before he had to sell up, in his Natural History of Wiltshire, "Quare, if it would not bee the better way to send our wooll beyond the sea again, as in the time of the staple? For the Dutch and French doe spin finer, work cheaper and die better. Our cloathiers combine against the wooll-masters, and keep their spinners but just aloive: they steal hedges, spoil coppices, and are trained up as nurseries of sedition and rebellion."

20 So Supple pp 210–1.

21 This had a beneficial aspect, too, since lighter woollens sold well in the newer, warmer export markets, though not of course in tropical areas.

22 See ODNB "Sir Thomas Gresham" p.5.

23 Official Exchangers had been in operation for a brief period in 1576: see Supple p.189.

24 See Supple p.208.

25 As to which see below and Appendix E.

26 Similar thinking perhaps underlies the modern UK Government schemes for "export credits".

27 For a brief overview, see Appendix E.

28 though James I did seriously consider appointing "official exchangers", to be chosen by Sanderson, as late as 1622: see CSPD 1619–22 p.417.

29 See APC 1619–21 p.393 and Supple p.186ff., who describes the majority of the Committee – Sanderson, Malynes and Maddison- as "adhering to what might be called the conspiratorial view of the economics of exchange rates".

30 See, for example, CSP Domestic 1629–31 p.423.

31 She had already been presented with the first terrestrial globe by Molyneux, the maker, some months before, at Greenwich.

32 See Prince Henry.

33 See Prince Henry, passim.

34 See ODNB "Edward Wright".

Chapter 6 – Marriage and Family

1 From his petition to Star Chamber c.1613: STAC 8/260/4.

2 Ibid.

3 While he confirms the quick transformation from friend to money-box, Sir William seems to have "telescoped" the timing on two matters (i) we are dealing here with the years after Sanderson's marriage (in 1584): the affair with Bess was some years later, and their secret marriage took place only in 1591 (ii) the £4000 debt emerged much later, from the settlement of accounts in 1595. Sir William, writing in 1656 was, not surprisingly, resentful of Ralegh's contribution to his father's financial disaster.

4 It was probably in 1592 that the Sandersons twice entertained the Queen at the Newington Butts house, when she was presented by Sanderson with Molyneux's terrestrial and celestial globes.

5 One son, Drake, being christened at Leyton in 1593.

6 See HL/PO/JO/10/1/154 and 155: it looks as though Sir William had to sort matters out.

7 See An Answer.

8 In 1633 the Russian assault on Smolensk, held by the Poles, was repulsed. Leslie was a fellow mercenary from the well-known Fife family. The Sandersons complained without success to the Office of Arms about the alleged murder: see SP80/9 folio 8.

9 No Sanderson is named in the inventory of Weymouth's voyage.

Part Two – Best Friend and Honorary Treasurer

1   See below p.54.

2   For Harriot see p.xiff above.

Chapter 7 – John Davis and the North West Passage

1   See HV III 33ff.

2   The account of the first voyage, written by John Janes, claims that Sanderson introduced John Davis to the investors: see HV III 120 though Ruth McIntyre suggests that the introduction might have been by Adrian Gilbert or by Ralegh: see McIntyre Article p.189.

3   Sir William, writing some 80 years later, in An Answer, thought there were two ships named "Sunshine" and "Rainbow".

4   See HV…Hakluyt describes him as " a man of good observation, imployed in the same (i.e. the last voyage of Cavendish) and many other voyages".

5   "Besides his travaile which was not small, hee became the greatest adventurer with his purse": quoted in Markham p.1.

6   WHD, reprinted in Markham p. 207–8.

7   See further p.49 below.

8   The story has recently been told in full by Samuel Bawlf in his "The Secret Voyage of Sir Francis Drake", though reservations have been expressed as to the accuracy of Bawlf's detailed description of Drake's coure up thre West coast of Canada.

9   Though this may have been intended for goldmining rather than colonisation.

10   See below, p.58ff.

11   A league at sea was 3.18 nautical miles, usually rounded to three nautical miles.

12   SeeWHD, Markham p.207.

13   See Markham p.xix.

14   See Cotton, minute for 19th April 1586.

15   WHD, Markham p.209.

16   "Our two barks for their fishing voyage, and my self in the pinnesse for the discovery": see Davis' Traverse Book i.e. his log, for 21st June 1587, Markham p.52.

17   From WHD see Markham p.210.

18   See Traverse Book, Markham p.55.

19   WHD, Markham p. 210.

20   It appears that Thomas Harriot independently invented a similar backstaff, but, as with many of his ideas and inventions, because he did not "publish" he failed to get the credit.

21   See Davis' letter to Sanderson of 14th.October 1586 quoted in Markham p.32, "I hope I will find favour with you to see your card (Markham suggests that this

refers to a new chart prepared for Sanderson). I pray God it be so true as the card shall be which I will bring to you: and I hope in God, that your skill in navigation shall be gainfull unto you , although, at the first, it hath not proved so".
22 See WHD, Markham p.215ff.

Chapter 8 – The Roanoke Settlement

1   See above p.37ff.
2   See Raleigh and Marlowe p.294.
3   Described above p.13–14.
4   See further Raleigh and Marlowe, Chapter 17, from which these extracts are taken.
5   Raleigh and Marlowe p.312.
6   See below Chapter 17.
7   A very readable up-to-date narrative of the Roanoke settlement is in Elizabeth.
8   Rosalind Davies takes the view that Harriot and Ralegh must "share the blame" for this distortion; see Davies Paper.
9   See Cotton p.81.
10 This was Sir Thomas Smythe, senior, known as "Customer Smythe": see RV p.544.
11 The agreement is printed in RV p.569.
12 See RV p.712n.
13 See Cotton p.80 "I think we may infer…that he was anything but a favourite with them".
14 See below Chapter 14.
15 See Cambridge History of the British Empire 1960 I. p.56–7.

Chapter 9 – The Munster Plantation

1   This chapter draws on "The Munster Plantation" by Michael McCarthy-Morrogh.
2   See, for example, Canny, chapters 2, Edmund Spencer's contribution and 3.1, The Munster Plantation, The Theory.
3   See Munster Plantation p.119ff.
4   See Munster Plantation p.249.
5   See Ralegh p.152–3.
6   So Munster Plantation p.124.
7   Munster Plantation p.124; see also Sir William's mention of his father's Irish land-holding in An Answer, though he implies, incorrectly, that his father had inherited rather than buying it.

8   See Canny p.308ff.

9   See Bess p.251ff.

10   See above p.52.

11   Some of the land passed by marriage to the Cavendish family.

Chapter 10 – Molyneux's Globes

1   Quoted in RV p.513.

2   Wallis 1989 article p.94.

3   Though he had been to sea: see below p.61 and made precision instruments.

4   A good account is given in Mercator.

5   If read literally, the Memorandum by a Freind, probably written in 1626 and usually attributed to Sir William, might assign that role to Sanderson himself, "Hee invented, made, printed, and published the great Spheares and Globes, both Celestiall and Terrestriall, being the first soe published in Christendome, for the honour of his countrie, and good of the Schollers, Gentrys, and mariners of the same". This wide-ranging attribution, however, seems to be to stem from excessive enthusiasm, as does the error about "the first in Christendome".

6   See below p.64.

7   See ODNB "Molyneux".

8   See CSP Domestic 1574–80 p.339.

9   See Robert Hues, Tractatus, Hakluyt Socy. Vol 79 1889 p.xxx; but there is doubt about the Cavendish voyage: see Wallis 1951 article p.283.

10   See, below, p.63.

11   Thomas Harriot seems to have been covering the same ground "in parallel".

12   Later, Wright became tutor to James I's eldest son, Prince Henry: see further below p.29.

13   See WHD, at Markham p.211.

14   The Molyneux celestial globe had somewhat less impact than the terrestrial: its practical uses were fewer, and it did not carry comparable dramatic new material.

15   The Molyneux terrestrial globe may have been too large for this: see David. W. Waters in Drake p.20.

16   For example, Queen Elizabeth in the Plimpton Sieve portrait, the Armada portrait, the Rainbow portrait; the Lane portrait of Drake; the Zuccari portrait of Ralegh.

17   Or 662 mm. Hues gives the diameter of the larger globes as 2' 2": see Wallis 1951 Article p.282.

18   Wallis 1951 Article p.284–5. The estimated cost of £20 for a pair of the larger globes may be open to question: The Warden of All Souls, according to the College accounts, paid only around £2 for a pair, although a further amount over £3 was paid for their embellishment and installation. Again, the pair of larger

globes purchased by Sir Thomas Bodley for his library cost nearly £20 but this included sumptuous gilding and painting: see Craster Article F.

19 See Wallis 1951 article p.282.

20 Petruccio Ubaldini: see below p.63.

21 See Crino/Wallis article, p.14.

22 See Bawlf p.240: Bawlf states that this first terrestrial globe showed Drake's true course to Nova Albion around 50 N and that it therefore had to be amended twice to conform with the requirement for secrecy.

23 See Forman. He in fact had extensive clinical experience, and wide interests outside medicine. His practice of astrology was shared by most doctors of the time and other eminent scientists indulged in what are now regarded as "fringe activities", astrology, necromancy, alchemy and so on, for example Dr John Dee and Sir Isaac Newton]   See ODNB "Molyneux" p.2 and the Crino/Wallis article pp.13–14.

24 Forman may have been introduced to Molyneux by Sanderson, since Forman was tenant of a large orchard owned by Sanderson in Lambeth: see SPD C54/1862.

25 See the Crino/Wallis article on which this account is based.

26 than English.

27 The Crino/Wallis article p.16 refers to a painting in the Pinocoteca Nazional, Siena which portrays the Queen with her Court, which may reflect the Greenwich presentation. In the background there is a large terrestrial globe inscribed "Tutto Vedo et Molto *Mancha*" – I see everything and much *is lacking*. The word in italics are added, having been omitted in the Crino/Wallis article.

28 Alluding to the King's Emblem, a Spanish Genet: Genets resemble wild cats but are in fact related to the mongoose family: to-day they are mainly found in Africa, but were in the past also living in south Europe, where a few survive e.g. in the national park in South West Spain.

29 Sir William was about six years old in 1592 and may well have been presented to the Queen, though he does not mention that he witnessed either visit – as he does on other occasions.

30 "The Crest is not fitt for so mean a person but rather for one that possessed the whole wourlde". The archivist to the College, however, attributes the disparaging comments to backbiting among the heralds – Dethick was unpopular with his colleagues – rather than to their view of the Sandersons as social climbers: private communication July 2004.

31 Reproduced in Appendix B.

32 Ibid.

33 See p.93.

34 See this page.

35 The Crawshaw/Middle Temple pair appears to be such a sale.

36 See the discussion in the Wallis 1955 article p.310.

37 See Wallis 1955 article p.305.

38 See Wallis 1951 article p.280.
39 See Wallis 1951 article pp. 280–2; Wallis 1955 article pp.304–7; Wallis 1989 article p.96.
40 See Wallis 1951 article p.288.
41 See the Crino/Wallis article p.15.
42 See Wallis 1951 article p.280.
43 See BL MS. Julius C.V.fol.385 undated.
44 In late 1592 or 1593: see the Wallis 1951 article p.280.
45 See Champion Article.
46 See Use of the Globes, 1602.
47 Act III Scene II line 77ff.
48 Act III, Scene II.
49 See Wallis 1951 article p.288.
50 p.73.
51 "The use of both the Globes, Celestial and terrestrial, most plainly delivered in form of a dialogue.".
52 It seems clear that this work owed something to the collaboration of Thomas Harriot: see Harriot p.201.
53 See Wallis 1955 article p.311.

Part Three – Trust Betrayed and an Obstinate Loyalty

Chapter 11 – South America: the Search for El Dorado

1 See Salisbury MS Part IV p.329. Sir William, writing in An Answer 64 years later, mistakenly stated that Sanderson was one of the Commissioners and represented the Queen. Sir William obviously got muddled, since the Commissioners had to decide on the allocation of the spoils while the "representatives" were advancing the claims of their "clients"; thus no individual could perform both functions.
2 See Youings pp.78–9.
3 Aubrey pp. 416–7.
4 See the illustration on the back cover, which is based on a modern watercolour, held in the Sherborne Castle archives, by Jim Gibb, a local historian. This attractive painting is of particular interest since its historical accuracy is based on (i) a 1600 plan held in the archives of Hatfield House and (ii) a careful examination by the artist of the Castle when it was stripped of its rendering for repairs, which revealed the details of the original building, before the addition of four wings (in the same style) by Sir John Digby after his acquisition in 1617.
5 See The Golden Man, passim.
6 Berrio was captured by Ralegh in Trinidad in 1595, as described below.

7   Another account states that he was freshly covered with gold dust every day.

8   An explanation is offered at p.263ff. of The Golden Man.

9   In 1584, 1585–1588 (28 months) and 1591–2.

10 Since Harris witnessed the vital formal release document handed by Ralegh to Sanderson –see below.

11 From his petition to Star Chamber: see STAC 8/260/4.

12 This is established because the amount challenged as being insufficiently accounted for – namely £60,000 – exceeded the cost of the Manao/El Dorado expedition on its own, thought to be about £40,000.

13 Almost certainly, as mentioned above, he had not foreseen that in granting an absolute release to Ralegh and Bess Sanderson would "except out of it" the money which he had just borrowed and handed over to Ralegh.

14 See Appendix D for a "guesstimated" cashflow for Ralegh's operations down to 1595.

15 See Bess p.91.

16 See Harriot p.202.

17 Ibid.

18 There were some doubts expressed as to exactly where these valuables had come from.

19 So Raleigh p.262.

20 See the analysis in The Creature in the Map.

21 i.e. she also has access to her husband's money.

22 an escheator was the officer responsible for seizing property which reverted to the feudal lord on intestacy but the word was used figuratively to describe a plunderer.

23 See Merry Wives I. iii. 64–5.

245 See Salisbury MS XIV 172. 16.

256 See 1421 p.116ff. Darwin fund a skeleton of a mylodon in Patagonia in 1834.

Chapter 12 – The Curious Incident of the Dog in the Night-Time

1   See Youings p.235 n.14.

2   See Raleigh p.401.

3   See Silver Blaze by Arthur Conan Doyle. "Is there any incident to which you would wish to draw my attention? To the curious incident of the dog in the night-time. The dog did nothing in the night-time. That was the curious incident" remarked Sherlock Holmes.

4   Although it occurred a little later, in 1602, the disposal of the Irish property, which was not inherited but had been purchased by Sanderson himself, might be related to this cash problem.

5   It is possible that this change of circumstances, avoiding a personal demand on Ralegh, made it more palatable for Sanderson to move at last.

6   See STAC 8/260/4.

7   Following his attainder Ralegh does not seem, strictly speaking, entitled to give such instructions.

8   See, for example ODNB article "Sanderson", "unwise investments in voyages and properties, as well as expensive litigation".

9   See Appendix A.

10   Sanderson's involvement in mining is described, as far as the limited facts permit, below at p.95ff.

11   In 1610 there were no bankruptcy or "administration" arrangements available, under which the claims of creditors might be dealt with in an orderly manner.

12   See SPD C2/Jas I/56/3.

13   See below.

14   See Minutes for 14th. August 1598.

15   See Fishmongers' Court Minutes Vol I, Back Pages.

16   See HFC XIII p.168n. For the enhanced arms, see p.65.

17   They are held respectively by the RGS and the BL.

18   For example, with the RGS.

19   See p.xiii.

20   Both Harriot and Hues in due course became "gentlemen pensioners" of Northumberland, though Harriot continued to work actively on Raleigh's financial and general affairs.

21   Identified by Anna Beer as Edmund Lascelles, a "minor courtier" implicated in the Gunpowder plot and another plot to kill King James and Cecil: see Bess p.169–170.

22   Anna Beer presents a case for Lascelles being the father of Bess's baby and for the move to join Ralegh in the Tower being a "cover" for the pregnancy: see Bess pp. 169–170. However, James I turned away when Carew was introduced to him as a young man, seeing the ghost of Ralegh: see Ibid. p.244, Ralegh p.561, and Bess herself worked for many years to have Carew "restored in blood".

23   See CSPD 1603–10 p.76, para 30. Since Ralegh had settled Sherborne on Wat after his own death, only his life interest had been forfeited to the Crown following his conviction for treason: this settlement was later to be declared ineffective, so that Sherborne went to the Crown in toto.

24   See Youings p.310.

25   See below p.102.

26   This quite generous settlement was, apparently, negotiated from an initially lower figure by Bess personally: see Bess pp.189–190.

27   Sir Roy Strong points out that there is no positive evidence that Ralegh ever met the Prince, but in view of their wide shared interests, and the Prince's concern about Ralegh's liberty and his ownership of Sherborne , it looks very likely that they did: see Prince Henry.

28 See above p.36–9.
29 Quoted in Ralegh p.416.

Chapter 13 – A Mining Disaster

1 Senior, "Customer Smythe".
2 See the discussion above at p..]
3 See BL Loan No.16.
4 See Donald pp192–3; STAC 5/B74/39 & B 105/8; STAC 5/B28/35, B103/1 & B68/33 &
5 See Derbyshire Lead Industry p.179.
6 Donald pp. 163, 170, 171.

Chapter 14 – In Chancery and Star Camber

1 See Harriot and the Shirley Article.
2 However, as will appear, we part company with Dr Shirley on the *evaluation* of the factual and legal points, and, particularly on his final, overall judgment "All the extant evidence is before the reader, and it is he who must assume the role of the judge in the controversy between Sir Walter Raleigh, Knight, and William Sanderson, gent." .
3 Even to-day, witnesses tend to swear and sign affidavits, without too much careful examination, simply because they have been drafted by a lawyer, however partisan.
4 See Appendix D for an estimated cashflow.
5 See above p.78.
6 i.e. subject to conditions.
7 to Ralegh.
8 See further, Limitation, Part 4, "Limitation in Equity".
9 Since 1875 there are no separate Chancery Courts in England and all English courts apply both the legal rules and the "principles of equity".
10 He also built Montacute House in Somerset.
11 See further ODNB "Sir Edward Phelips".
12 These signatures are omitted on the only surviving copy.
13 See Shirley Article.
14 Their reports are in Appendix H .
15 See, for example, Ralegh's letter to Salisbury 12/13 November 1595: Youings p.126.
16 John Meere had of course been caught, by Ralegh himself, "practising" Ralegh's signature: see below.

17 See Dorset Elizabethans p.277ff.

18 For example, letter198 in Youings.

19 See Bess p. 190–1.

20 Although the price was payable by instalments the deal had been done in 1602 before Elizabeth died and James I moved against Ralegh.

21 See Bess p.232.

22 Formal questions to be answered on oath.

23 See above p...

24 See above p...

25 see SPD C4/372.

26 Noted in the Davies Paper.

27 The text is printed in Appendix F.

28 See Youings p.321 n.9.

29 That is the Court official to administer the interrogatories to the witnesses.

30 in 1604.

31 in 1611.

32 See above p.81.

33 Sanderson's petition to Star Chamber mentions that the proceedings in Chancery were commenced "at the direction of" Raleigh: strictly speaking, therefore, Raleigh directed the administrators to act in breach of the trust which Salisbury, on Royal authority, had established. "Do not pay his debt under the "trust" – commence proceedings to frighten him off". While necessarily speculative, this explanation appears to fit the circumstances; and this kind of legal tactic seems to have been quite common.

34 See the discussion below at p.116ff.

35 If the ODNB account is correct, perhaps the necessary funds were found by the Exchequer, on the basis that the value of the real and personal property which eventually reached the Royal treasury, under Raleigh's attainder, had, all along, been wrongfully inflated by the amount of Sanderson's unpaid debts; but there is no record of this having occurred.

Chapter 15 – Debtors' Prisons

1 A recognisance was a formal promise to pay registered with the court – it was a way of increasing the return to the lender without falling foul of the very complicated laws on "usury": as to which see further Appendix F.

2 He seems to have been appointed around 1615: see E 215/1680.

3 See Calendar of the Records of the Fishmongers' Company II. 555. 24th. April 1620.

Part Four – Judgement Deferred

Chapter 16 – End of the Story?

1   See above pp.123–4.

2   No trace has been found of the burial. Sir William's description suggests St. Mary le Strand alias Savoy: the Savoy Chapel seems less appropriate as it was non-parochial. However St. Mary's was demolished by 1548 by the Duke of Somerset to make way for Somerset House and no replacement was built until 1717. During the 1548–1717 period the parishioners of St. Mary's were distributed in a somewhat haphazard way between St. Clement Danes, St. Martin's in the Fields and the Savoy Chapel.

3   The evidentiary weight of Sir William's account is discussed in Appendix A.

Chapter 17 – Final Verdict

1   See pp.123–4.

2   As with the Thames Street property he would have had to act jointly with his heir, Raleigh Sanderson].

3   It is possible, too, that Sanderson, and perhaps also his wife, were uncomfortable that the stock of cash destined to support Ralegh, Bess and Wat should be depleted by paying the £4000 owed.

4   See above, p.83.

5   For example Sanderson's "papers" on foreign exchange, usury &c.have been frequently attributed to Sir William and the 17th. century engraving of Sir William (reproduced at p.. below) was used to illustrate an article on Sanderson: see The Geographical Journal Vol. XXI, June 1903 p.597; again, Sanderson was not considered worthy of inclusion in the DNB.

6   Published 1868: see p.459.

7   Published 1900 see p.19.

8   See the discussion at pp.118–9 in Appendix A.

9   Shirley Guyana Article.

10 See "Davies Paper".

11 The allegation that Sanderson was "in arrears" with cash from licensing the import and retailing of wines is made in the biographies of Ralegh by Edward Edwards and of Harriot by Henry Stevens: it appears to be based, without attribution, on a piece of personal invective in the anonymous Observations: see p..above. It is suggested that the allegation cannot stand and needs to be reconsidered.

APPENDIX A – Sir William's Biographical Notes on Sanderson

1   See Pepys 9th/10th May 1660. Pepys authorised a passage for him.

2   See ODNB "Sanderson, Sir William".

3   Carew Ralegh's role in relation to "Observations" may need to be reconsidered, since there appears to have been a relationship by marriage between him and Sir William's wife, Dame Bridget. Carew Raleigh married his daughter Anne to Sir Peter Tyrell of Hanslope (1st Baronet) as his second wife. Sir Peter was the younger son of Sir Thomas Tyrell of Hanslape and Throp, one of whose sisters was Bridget Tyrell. Bridget was thus aunt to Sir Peter and when she married Sir William Sanderson became aunt by marriage to Anne, daughter of Carew Ralegh. See BEB 1844. Whether this relationship would have prevented Carew Ralegh from writing or contributing to Observations is for consideration; perhaps Carew Ralegh was content to shelter behind a cover of anonymity, or perhaps in any case he simply supplied ammunition for another writer.

4   This claim is made by a number of other Sandersons as well.

5   The text of the Memoir is conveniently printed in RV p.576.

6   See above p.22.

7   See Appendix E.

8   See above p.21.

9   See CSPD 1619–23 p.542 (Usury); CSPD 1625–6 p.513 (Royal Exchanger); CSPD 1629–31 p.423 (apparently following on the preceding paper: Commerce and a State Merchant).

APPENDIX D – "Honorary Treasurer" to Sir Walter Ralegh

1   As to which see Appendix E.

2   See further Appendix E.

3   See his petition to the Star Chamber, discussed at p.80.

APPENDIX E – Lending and Usury

1   For a fuller account, see "God and the Moneylenders" on which this summary is based.

2   See God and the Moneylenders, Chapter 5, for detailed descriptions and reported examples.

APPENDIX G – Gwyana/Guyana – Use as a place name

1   Dr. John Shirley in the Huntington Library Quarterly XIII (1949) p.67.
2   1550–60: F 1540, P/14 (12v).

Index

undertakes commercial
arbitration and diplomatic
missions 18, 20
serves on Privy Council
committees 117
selects investment of national
importance 6
heraldic arms embellished by
Queen's order 9, 65, 65★
Interests and skills
applied sciences ("arts") 17
economics 21 ff
a mercantilist 27
favours exchange control 27
makes a valuable (but
unidentified)
contribution to the Royal
Exchequer 21
mining and metallurgy 19, 95ff.
cartography and navigation 19
falls into debt 88 ff.
mining losses 90, 85 ff.
imprisoned for debt 116 ff., 95
ff.
collaboration with R viii. ix
private banker 17
treasurer/finance manager ix,
Appendix D
provides ships 59
obstinate loyalty" after 1595
quarrel 123-4
Hounslow Heath support viii,
ix, 88, 13

visits to R in prison 94
helps Bess join R in the Tower
93
making up to Prince Henry 28,
94
corroborating R's travellers'
tales 86
For individual projects see specific
subjects e.g.El Dorado,
Munster, Roanoke
Sarmiento Don Pedro 75
Schutz Christopher 07
Shelbury John 81, 89, 106, 107, 109
Sherborne Lodge started 1594
Skinners Company 7
Smythe Sir Thomas ("Customewr"
Smythe) 50
Snedall Hugh 12
Social Rank importance of 8, 9, 125
Staper Richard 20
Ubaldini Petruccio 63 ff.
Van Lore Peter xi
Waad Sir Wi;lliam vii
Walsingham Sir Francis 38
Watts John Sir 20, 50
White John 49-50, 54
Woollen Exports 1500-1630 21 ff.
22★
Wright Edward 13, 59 ff.
Zouche Sir John of Codno 97 ff.